T0115094

EXPLORING HEBREWS

A DEVOTIONAL COMMENTARY

Ashley Day

authorHOUSE®

AuthorHouse™
1663 Liberty Drive
Bloomington, IN 47403
www.authorhouse.com
Phone: 1-800-839-8640

Published by AuthorHouse 2/5/2013

ISBN: 978-1-4817-1120-3 (sc)
ISBN: 978-1-4817-1119-7 (hc)
ISBN: 978-1-4817-1118-0 (e)

Library of Congress Control Number: 2013901452

"The sower sows the Word" (Mark 4:14)

Seed-Time Ministries, Inc.,

5080 N. 4th Street,

Coeur d'Alene ID 83815

Tel. (208)765-3714

http://www.seedtime.net

admin@seed-time.org

TABLE OF CONTENTS

Acknowledgment

This book is produced with grateful thanks to the many faithful friends who support the work of Seed-Time Ministries with their prayers and financial gifts. Without their faithfulness this ministry would cease to exist.

INTRODUCTION

Nobody knows for certain who wrote the letter to the Hebrews. Many scholars (such as Arthur Pink and the early Catholics) believe Paul was the author. Others claim it was written by Timothy or Barnabas. Some even suggest Aquila and Priscilla were the writers. Still others (such as Martin Luther and R.C. Lenski) believe that Apollos wrote it. But despite the learned theories, which claim to "prove" the author's identity, none succeeds, and the fact remains that despite two thousand years of scholarship, nobody knows who actually penned these immortal words.

Even if we knew the author's identity, the knowledge would not help us very much. It would not change one word of the letter, nor make it more effective. We shall therefore not waste time following rabbit trails in this volume, but will instead concentrate on what the letter itself has to say. We shall seek to learn from it, bearing in mind that although God has not revealed the identity of the human author, the letter was clearly written by divine appointment. *"All Scripture is God-breathed"* (2 Timothy 3:16) and *"The prophecy came not in old time by the will of man: but holy men of God spoke as they were moved by the Holy Ghost"* (2 Peter 1:21).

Another unanswered question concerns the identity of those to whom the letter was addressed. Clearly it was written to a group of Jewish Christians. There is nothing in the letter to suggest that Gentiles were addressed. It is also clear from chapter 13 that the writer was addressing a specific organized group. He was hoping to visit them soon in the company of Timothy (verse 23) and he called upon the believers to obey those who had the rule over them (verse 17). He sent these leaders special greetings (verse 24). The location of the church is also unknown. Various theories have been offered but none gives proof of its claim.

Most Christian bodies at that time consisted of a mixture of Gentile and Jewish converts but this group appears have been comprised purely of Jewish Christians.

The problem addressed by the letter is that of apostasy. Within the body of believers, there was a movement toward forsaking the Christian faith and returning to their former Judaism. Members of the church had suffered limited persecution due to the fact that they had sympathized with some of their number, who had been imprisoned (10:32-34). So far, none of them had suffered martyrdom (12:4). In his letter, the writer strives to convince them of the riches of their faith in Christ and the foolishness of reverting to their Old Testament practices, which were but the shadow of the true Gospel of salvation.

Soon after the turn of the 20th century, Philip Mauro pointed out in his book "God's Pilgrims" that this letter was addressed to "Hebrews" and that the man most frequently and prominently mentioned in it is Abraham, who is specifically designated *"the Hebrew"* in Genesis 14:13. Hebrew scholars tell us that the word, *"Hebrew"* signifies *"one who passes through"*. We may therefore regard a Hebrew as a "traveler" and certainly the message of this letter is for those who are "travelers" in this age; those who have no continuing city but who seek one to come. The message is not for Israelites, who have a place in the world and a mission to the nations. Much less, is it for unconverted persons, or for such as make a mere profession of Christianity. It is written expressly for the *"sons of God"*, the *"holy brethren, partakers of the heavenly calling"*, for the *"heirs of salvation"*, who have access to God through the blood of Christ. In particular, this letter has a message for those of God's children who are in a backward or immature state, whose great need is to grow in grace and in the knowledge of the Lord Jesus Christ. Abraham was not an Israelite. Nor were those who preceded him. Jacob (Israel) had not yet been born.

In the Bible, God provides two types of blessing to those who trust Him – *gifts* and *rewards*. The gifts are unilateral and irrevocable. We can do nothing to merit them and nothing that would cause them to be taken away. They are based solely on the finished work of Jesus Christ and are given freely to people who, though still sinners by nature, have turned to Christ for mercy and have trusted Him for forgiveness and eternal life. Salvation and its attendant certainties are gifts from God. They are given without conditions and are already ours -- in the present tense.

When Paul addressed the Ephesians he wrote, "God *has blessed us* with all spiritual blessings in Christ; He *has chosen us* to be holy and without blame before Him; He *has predestined us* to be adopted into His family; He *has redeemed and forgiven us;* He *has sealed us* with the promised Holy Spirit and He *has given us* an inheritance" (Ephesians 1:3-14). All those wonderful blessings are unilateral gifts and have already been given to us. They do not depend in any way upon our performance for their fulfillment. We have them now; they are already ours.

Rewards, on the other hand, are conditional. They depend on how we build upon the foundation of our faith in Christ. 1 Corinthians 3 makes it very clear that at the judgment seat of Christ, the believer's work on earth will be evaluated. Unlike gifts (which are present) rewards are future. They will be the result of faithfulness and perseverance in this life. Whereas all Christians have the gifts, by reason of their salvation, not all Christians will receive rewards. The group to which this epistle was written were obviously discouraged and in danger of giving up. This letter was written to exhort them to keep on keeping on, to keep *"looking unto Jesus, the Author and finisher of faith."* Their danger was not that they might lose their salvation. That was not possible, since salvation is a free gift based upon the merits of Jesus Christ. Their danger was that they might lose their rewards, just as a whole generation of Israelites lost theirs in the wilderness, through unbelief.

By analogy, the ancient Israelites did not need to be redeemed in the wilderness. They were already redeemed by the blood of the Passover lamb. However, they allowed the reward for faithfulness to slip through their fingers because they failed to trust the Lord in the difficult times. Similarly, the letter to the Hebrews does not deal with salvation, in the sense that John spoke of it. Hebrews assumes that its readers are born again. The writer deals with salvation in the sense that Peter uses the word in his first epistle, where he writes to believers "who *are kept by the power of God unto salvation, ready to be revealed in the last time.*" (1 Peter 1:5). Salvation, in that passage, is not the salvation of the soul. That was already fact. Peter was addressing those who had received all the present blessings listed in Ephesians 1, and now looked forward to the future fulfillment of their faith. As Christians, we have been blessed with all spiritual blessings in heavenly places but we still dwell in mortal bodies, living out our faith in a world that hates God.

"Reality", to our mortal senses, means the material world, because we have never experienced anything else. The future is seen only in our imagination. One day, faith will turn to sight and reality will suddenly become the heavenly realm. That is the salvation to which Peter refers and it is also the vision which the writer to the Hebrews presents, to encourage those whose feet are dragging. There are dangers in this life, and many enemies. If we once take our eyes off the glorious goal which is set before us, we might well sink into discouragement.

To quote Mauro again: "The dangers against which we are warned are those to which God's own people are exposed. Little is said of the doom awaiting those who have rejected God's grace, and who are lost eternally; but much is said of the loss which the people of God may incur by failing to take heed of the things the Lord Himself "began to speak." That the people of God can, by flagrant disobedience, bring upon themselves great suffering and loss, is clearly set forth in many Scriptures. But it is equally clear that they themselves cannot be lost."

So here we are, travelers (*Hebrews,* if you like), and here is a portion of God's Word which is designed to encourage and strengthen us in our faith. Except for a few isolated passages, it is not addressed to non-believers, who need to be saved. Other Scriptures speak to them. This letter is addressed to believers who are discouraged. Perhaps you find yourself among their number. The way has become hard and you feel tired, discouraged and defeated. You might even have secretly wondered if it is all worth the effort. God doesn't seem to come through for you; prayer doesn't seem to work; your heart is hard and dry, as if the moisture has been drained out of it. You continue to go through the motions because you know you should, but the joy is missing. Well, here you have a letter addressed to you. It presents Jesus Christ in all His glory and power. He is presented as our high priest, intercessor, brother and example, one who understands how we feel. It exhorts us to raise ourselves from apathy and mediocrity; to lift up the hands that hang down and the feeble knees; to draw near with a true heart, in full assurance of faith; to hold fast the profession of our faith without wavering; to run with patience the race that is set before us, and to labor to enter into the rest of God. The key to it all is Christ.

When reading this volume it is important that you carefully read the Scripture verse before going on to the text. The exposition which follows is tied to the verse that precedes it and may not be as beneficial if the Scripture is omitted.

The introduction to Hebrews in the Life Application Bible reads, "Whatever you are considering as the focus of life, Christ is better. He is the perfect revelation of God, the final and complete sacrifice for sin, the compassionate and understanding mediator, and the only way to eternal life. Read Hebrews and begin to see history and life from God's perspective. Then give yourself unreservedly and completely to Christ. Don't settle for anything less."

CHAPTER 1

The Word has spoken

Verses 1-2:

"God, who at various times and in different ways spoke in time past to the fathers by the prophets. 2 has in these last days spoken to us by His Son. . "

If we were to take away the descriptive clauses from the opening statement, we would be left with three words: *"God has spoken."* God, who is in heaven, has spoken to men who are upon the earth. That immediately raises several questions: a) What did He say? b) When did He say it? c) How did He speak? d) Why did He speak? and e) How do we know that it was God who spoke? Obviously, some of these questions are answered in the text. In the past, God spoke to the fathers (the fathers of the Jewish nation) through the prophets. A prophet is *"one who speaks forth."* Various men were raised by God and used as channels through whom He communicated with His people. These prophets were tools in God's hand. Peter wrote that they were moved by the Holy Spirit. They could not help speaking.

The prophet, Balaam, even tried to prophesy falsely, but discovered that he was unable to do so. The prophets' words were not their own; they belonged to God. Jeremiah was reluctant to become a prophet. He argued with God about his appointment, but to no avail. He was chosen to be a mouthpiece for God before he was born. So was John the Baptist, whom Jesus called *"the greatest of all the prophets."* These men provided a blaze of glory through the pages of the Old Testament. Moses, Elijah, Elisha, Isaiah, Jeremiah, Daniel and Ezekiel, to name but a few, were all used at sundry times by God to speak to the fathers. Always they pointed forward, toward a time when a greater communicator would occupy the stage of history.

The centuries passed; kingdoms rose and fell, and *"when the fullness of time had come, God sent forth His Son, made of a woman, made under the law, to redeem those who were under the law."* (Galatians 4:4-5). Consequently, the writer to the Hebrews was able to say: "(God) *in these last days, has spoken unto us by His Son."* This was an astounding statement. It was unimaginable that God's own Son should take His place in the society of men, rubbing shoulders with His own creation in the everyday bustle of humanity! But when Jesus was transfigured on the mountain, a bright light appeared to the disciples and a voice out of Heaven said, *"This is my beloved Son, in whom I am well pleased. Hear Him."* (Matthew 17:5) He was the eternal Word of God, the "express image of God's person." He came to communicate God's love to man, and to open the door through which sinful and guilty men and women might find forgiveness. God has spoken through His Son.

An important truth to bear in mind is that speaking is only 50% of true communication. Speaking, in itself, does not communicate truth. I could go out into the desert, or into an empty room, and speak, but I would not be communicating because nobody would hear me. In other words, 50% of communication is listening. Thus, I do not have to go into the desert in order *not* to communicate. All I need is an audience which does not want to hear what I say. Thus true communication demands two things: a speaker and a willing hearer. This is the precise area where the human race falls short. God spoke through the prophets to the fathers, but only a small percentage of the fathers was willing to listen. In response, God said through the prophet Isaiah:

> *"This is a rebellious people, lying children, children who will not hear the word of the Lord; who say to the seers, See not, and to the prophets, Prophesy not unto us right things, speak unto us smooth things, prophesy deceits. Get you out of the way, turn aside out of the path, cause the Holy One of Israel to cease before us."*

Then God spoke through His Son, and the people still refused to listen. *"We have no king but Caesar"*, they cried. Nevertheless, this verse says, "(God) *has spoken unto US through His Son."* The Word is forever personal and current. We could cluck pompously about the foolishness of the people at the time of the prophets, and in the time of Jesus, but unless we listen and take to heart what the Scriptures say to us today, we are equally as foolish as they were. Speaking is aimed at the will. Jesus said, "*He who hears these sayings of mine and does them, I will liken him to a wise man who built his house upon a rock.*" Blessings in abundance are contained in this letter to the Hebrews, but there are warnings also. If we accept the blessings we must also accept the warnings. We cannot select one and reject the other. That option is not given to us.

The supremacy of Christ

The remainder of verse 2 and verse 3 describe the majesty of this One, through whom God has spoken unto us.

> "*. . .whom He has appointed heir of all things, through whom also He made the worlds; 3 who, being the brightness of His glory and the express image of His person, and upholding all things by the word of His power, when He had by Himself purged our sins, sat down at the right hand of the Majesty on high.*"

Seven truths are embodied in this description, each one describing a facet of the supremacy of Jesus.

First, (at the end of verse 2): "*He is heir of all things.*" The word "heir" has a double significance. It speaks of both honor and legal title. An heir is someone who is appointed to receive property, title and estate from another. In this case, the appointed one is heir to the entire realm of Almighty God. The One upon whom the title and honor have been bestowed is obviously the man, Jesus. And since God lives and operates in eternity, rather than within the limits of time, the appointment was made in the endlessness of eternity, before the universe was created. Just as believers were chosen before the foundation of the world, and the Lamb was slain before the foundation of the world, so the Lord Jesus was appointed heir of all things before the foundation of the world.

The scope of Christ's title is absolute. He has been appointed heir of *all things.* That leaves nothing out. It includes things in Heaven and things on earth, visible and invisible, thrones, dominions, principalities and powers. It includes control of the universe and power over the forces of death. In all things, Jesus has been given the preeminence, because it pleased the Father that in Him should all fullness dwell. That is why the Lord Jesus was able to say to His disciples before He ascended into Heaven, *"All power is given unto me, in heaven and on earth."*

The wonderful truth is that we, as Christians, are all involved in this appointment. Romans 8:16 tells us *"The Spirit Himself bears witness with our spirit that we are the children of God."* That places us into God's family, through our identification with Christ. Then verse 17 continues: *"And if children, then heirs; heirs of God, and joint heirs with Christ."* In other words, we have entered into the inheritance that God has given to Jesus. The term *"co-heir"* does not indicate two different inheritances, as if Jesus had one and we another. It indicates inclusion in the *"all things"* that belong to Him, which makes us richer than the wealthiest person on earth!

Second, through Him God *"made the worlds."* The word translated *"worlds"* in that phrase is actually *"aiwn"* (*"ages"*), vast periods of time through which the created universe has come. Not only did the entire physical universe have a beginning but time and space had a beginning also. We must break away from the notion that in the beginning there were time and space and then God began to work. God always existed. He created time and space together with the material universe. He created the ages, and all things within them, through His Son. Of course, the man, Jesus, did not create the universe. He had a beginning, just like you and I did. He was conceived, carried and delivered like every other human being. But the Word, the Son, who *became* the Lord Jesus, had always been. As Isaac Watts wrote:

"Before the hills in order stood,
Or earth received her frame,
From everlasting, Thou art God,
To endless years the same."

God has always been there, in the three co-equal Persons of the Trinity. One Person was never more important, more powerful or more senior than the other two. If one side of a triangle were to be removed, it would cease to be a triangle and the same is true of God. John called the second Person of the Trinity "*The Word.*" He wrote at the opening of his Gospel: "*In the beginning was the Word, and the Word was with God, and the Word was God. . . All things were made by Him and without Him was not anything made that was made.*" Then he continued: "*And the Word became flesh and dwelt among us.*" In other words, the eternal Word of God, having created the universe from nothing, took upon Himself human flesh and became the Lord Jesus.

Third, He is "*the brightness of God's glory.*" He is essentially part of God's glory, not a product of it. Unlike the moon's light, which is reflected, the sun's energy and power comes from within itself. It produces its own glory. That is how it is with Christ. He does not simply reflect the glory of God, He IS the glory of God. As Wuest puts it, "*He is the out-raying of the divine glory.*" True, He did not appear this way when He walked this earth but looking back John wrote: "*We beheld His glory, the glory as of the only begotten of the Father.*" He saw the brightness of God's glory on the Mount of Transfiguration, but to most others Jesus was veiled in human flesh. In the opening chapters of the Revelation, John fell at His feet as one dead. The Lord's present glory was too much for human eyes. Now the veil has been removed and His glory has been revealed. When we see Him, we shall see Him as He is. More astounding still, we shall be like Him!

Fourth, (verse 3) He is "*the express image of His (God's) Person.*" The Greek word for "express image" is "*karakter.*" It refers to the impression left by a stamp or seal – an exact reproduction. Paul told the Colossians that Christ was "*the image of the invisible God.*" When you press a signet or seal into soft wax, you cannot see the signet because it is pointing way from you. It is pointing downwards and is invisible. But when you lift it up, the impression in the wax reveals, in perfect detail, the character of the seal. The very identity of the impression has been received from the signet and it is open to view. So it is with the Lord Jesus. He was able to say: "*I and my Father are one*", not merely one in philosophy, or one in purpose, but one in substance, essence and power.

The attributes of the three persons of the Trinity are identical. They are all the same God. However, only the Lord Jesus revealed the will and personality of the triune God to man. He alone took human form. As an illustration, suppose you found an ants' nest in the wrong place and you wanted to explain to the ants that it was not in their best interests to keep coming into your house. You could use various methods, but it would be difficult to communicate your will to them in a way they could understand. However, if you could become an ant for a minute or so, and reason with them in their own language and on their own wavelength, maybe something could be worked out to your mutual advantage. That is a silly illustration but it does serve to illustrate the gulf that the incarnation crossed – when God condescended to become one of His own creation.

Fifth, He is "*the upholder of all things.*" He is not only heir of all things and the creator of all things. He is also the upholder of all things. Colossians 1:17 says: "*He is before all things, and by Him all things consist (hold together).*" The only power that prevents the universe from disintegrating is the sustaining power of God. Here we are told that this immense power is vested in Jesus Christ. Notice that it is "the *Word* of His power." His word is the operating force. The Word of God is the will of God and His will is irresistible. Peter wrote of this in his second letter, when he referred to scoffers who would come in the last days and question God's integrity. He wrote:

> "*But this they are willingly ignorant of, that by the Word of God the heavens were of old, and the earth, standing out of the water and in the water. By the same Word the world that then was, being overflowed with water, perished. But the heavens and the earth which are now, by the same Word are kept in store, reserved unto flames against the day of judgment and perdition of ungodly men.*"

The universe was brought into existence from nothing by the Word of God. God commanded it and it happened. Then the Great Flood was brought about by the same Word of God. At the moment, this earth is preserved in its present condition, not by man (who seems to be doing his best to destroy it), but by the Word of God. And one day, God will say the Word and the earth will be destroyed by fire. This will take place at the close of the Millennium, before the new heaven and new earth are created.

Sixth, He "*by Himself purged our sins.*" A wonderful mixture of loneliness and triumph shines through that statement. He came into the world to carry out a mission which, without Him, was impossible. Man was incapable of purging his own sins. If it was ever to happen, somebody else had to do it for him. Who was there? No son of Adam could do it because man's predicament was created by Adam in the first place and now permeated the entire human race. Paul wrote: *"By one man sin entered into the world, and death by sin; so death passed upon all men."* The situation was hopeless. Then, in the fullness of time, God Himself took human flesh and, as Jesus, came into the world for this express purpose. He personally accepted their penalty and died under their weight, only to rise above them three days later. That was the triumph. But -- *"He by Himself purged our sins."* There is the loneliness. He died alone in the darkness, surrounded by the howling hosts of evil, in order that you and I might be redeemed. Nobody could help Him. Even the Father had to distance Himself. His was a personal sacrifice.

Seventh, He *"sat down at the right hand of the Majesty on high."* He made Himself of no reputation. He took upon Himself the form of a servant and became obedient unto death, even the death of the cross. *"But God has highly exalted Him and has given Him a name that is above every name, that at the name of Jesus every knee should bow, of things in heaven, and things on earth and things under the earth, and every tongue should confess that Jesus Christ is Lord, to the glory of God the Father."* Jesus is now sitting at the right hand of the majesty on high, His work completed. What a story! What a contrast between the prophets, who spoke in times past to the fathers, and the Son, who in these last days has spoken unto us! He is Lord of All, and He is our Savior. Here is a privilege given, regardless of race, education, social standing, talents or gifts. This One who holds the universe together with His Word says, *"Come to me, all you who labor and are heavy laden, and I will give you rest."* What fools we would be to neglect such an invitation!

Better than the angels

Verse 4:

"Having become so much better than the angels, as He has by inheritance obtained a more excellent name than they."

Since earliest times, men have had a fascination with angels. Stories abound involving the intervention or co-operation of angels in human affairs. Many are true; many are imaginary; some are satanic, but all are intriguing because they give evidence of a spirit world, which is there but just out of reach. In His wisdom, God chose to place a veil between the material world and the spirit world, a veil which human senses are not designed to penetrate. True to his nature, man endlessly searches for a way through the veil and often ends up confused and deluded as the result. I remember once seeing a television program devoted to angels. People were interviewed, stories were told, near-death experiences were recounted, and in all of them angels were given the place which rightfully belongs to Jesus Christ. Never once was His name mentioned, nor the problem of sin addressed. People ended up in glory through the mediation of angels, without any need of salvation. Some expected to become angels themselves after death. Theologians and scholars gave profound opinions (which had no reference to Scripture) and when the program ended we were left with a deep sense of pity for those who were so deceived by the enemy.

Yes, there are angels (both good and evil). The Scriptures abound with references to them. They are obviously endowed with super-natural powers and possess intelligence and abilities far beyond the scope of man. But they are all created beings, nevertheless, and as such they have defined limits. We should never be deceived into believing that angels are able to perform feats which only God can perform, or that they can bypass or influence the plan which God laid down in the beginning. They are not to be prayed to, or worshipped. The good angels are God's messengers, and as such they are devoted to doing only His will. The evil angels serve Satan and will eventually end up in the Lake of Fire.

In this section of Hebrews 1, we are dealing with the supremacy of Christ over all created beings. The seven attributes of the Lord Jesus in verses 2 and 3 provide the basis for the statement He made to His disciples: *"All power is given unto me in heaven and on earth."* This being so, He is infinitely superior, not only to the prophets (who spoke to the fathers in times past) but also to the angels.

The word *"made"* in verse 4, means *"became."* Jesus, the man, became *"so much better than the angels."* We must not lose sight of the fact that prior to His incarnation, He was the second Person of the Godhead. In that capacity He had always been *"better"*. The angels themselves were the work of His hands. However, He left His throne in glory and became a man, and for that brief period He voluntarily became *"lower than the angels,"* so that He could suffer death. He could not die while He remained in His eternal glory. Nor could He have died if He had become an angel. He deliberately became a man in order to win redemption for you and me. As a man He was rejected, scoffed at, beaten and nailed to a cross, but now (still a man) He is exalted far above the most powerful angel. He has taken His place at the right hand of God.

The angels have names but Jesus *"by inheritance has obtained a more excellent name than they."* His name is more than a means of identification. When the angel Gabriel appeared to Mary, to tell her about the child she would bear, he said: *"His name shall be called Jesus."* That was the name Joseph was to give Him at His birth. That is the name He carried throughout His life here on earth. But God has now given Him (by reason of His inheritance) a more excellent name. In Philippians 2:9, Paul explains that God *"has given Him a name* (correctly, *the* name) *that is above every name."* That name is not "Jesus." Joseph gave Him that. God has given Him another name that is above all others. In Revelation 19:12, John records: *"His eyes were as a flame of fire, and on His head were many crowns, and He had a name written, that no man knew, but He Himself."* Then we are told that *"at the name belonging to Jesus, every knee shall bow, and every tongue confess that Jesus Christ is Lord."*

The Scriptures give us some fairly clear insights into the character and ministry of angels. Psalm 103:20, for instance, says that they *"excel in strength, do the Lord's commandments and listen to His voice."* Matthew 25:31 says that they are *"holy"*, i.e. set apart for God's service. Matthew 28:3 says that *"their countenance is like lightening and their raiment white as snow."* Revelation 5:11 tells us that *"their number is without record and they continually surround the throne of God."*

Angels were prominent in John's vision of the end times, playing active roles in the unfolding drama of the ages. It was the angel Gabriel who told Mary about the child she would bear, and the same angel who told

Zacharias about the son of his old age. Angels heralded Christ's birth in Bethlehem, ministered to Him after His temptation in the wilderness, and strengthened Him in the Garden of Gethsemane. Angels troubled the waters at the pool of Bethesda, rolled away the stone from the empty tomb, announced Christ's resurrection to the women and His return to the disciples. Angels awoke Peter in his prison, caused the guards to sleep and the doors to open. When the Lord returns to set up His kingdom it will be the angels who will gather the elect from the four corners of the earth. We are told in the Scriptures that the law received by Moses was administered by the mediation of angels. According to Jude 9, there is one Archangel (Michael), who is called a "prince" in Daniel 10:21. It will be Michael's voice that will be heard when the Lord returns. There are special angels called cherubim and seraphim who surround the throne of God. Angels are very real and they not only have access into the presence of God in Heaven but play an intimate part in the administration of His kingdom.

Unfortunately, there is the negative type of angel also. Before he rebelled and fell, Lucifer was himself a high ranking angel. He was *"the cherub that covered,"* a creature of great beauty. He now commands a host of fallen angels, who were expelled from heaven with him. They are described in Ephesians 6 as *"principalities and powers, and the rulers of this world's darkness."* They do Satan's bidding just as the holy angels do God's bidding, confusing and deceiving men into believing error. Both Daniel and John speak of warfare in the heavens between the hosts of God and the forces of Satan. God is allowing them time now, but one day their rampage will come to an end. The wicked angels, along with Satan himself, are destined to be consigned to the Lake of Fire.

The people of Israel held the good angels in deep reverence, and rightly so. They carry with them the fragrance and holiness of God Himself and are obviously endowed with powers which (happily) are denied to men. Here we read that Christ, through whom the Father has spoken, is *"made so much better than the angels."* He has been proclaimed *"LORD"* in heaven and is recognized as *"Son"* by the Father.

Verse 5:

"For to which of the angels did He ever say: "You are My Son, today

I have begotten You"? And again: "I will be to Him a Father, and He shall be to Me a Son"?

The answer is obviously, "none." God never said anything like that to any angel, but He said it to Jesus. This is a deep and fascinating subject. Through the centuries there has been an ongoing theological battle over the true nature of the "Sonship" of Jesus. Very respectable men have taken opposing views. W.E. Vine, for instance, is on one side and Arthur Pink on the other. Both men are greatly respected and are recognized as being reliable teachers, but they disagree on this issue. The argument centers on the question of whether Christ was eternally the Son of God, or whether He became the Son of God when He was born into the human race. The second person of the Trinity always existed, as the Word of God. We know that. But was He always the "*Son*"? Some say "Yes" and others say "No." Personally, I feel more comfortable with the latter view, namely, that the perfect man, Jesus, became the "*only begotten Son of God*" when He was born into this world – when "*the Word became flesh and dwelt among us.*"

Nowhere do the Scriptures say that the "Son became flesh and dwelt among us." Here in verse 5, the writer to the Hebrews quotes Psalm 2:7, which says, "*You are my Son, THIS DAY have I begotten you.*" The word "*begotten*" means "*born.*" "*This day*" refers either to the day of Christ's birth or to the day of His baptism. Whichever it was, it was in time rather than in eternity. There are no days in eternity. The angel said to the shepherds: "*Unto you is born this day, in the city of David, a Savior, who is Christ, the Lord.*" In Luke 1:31, the angel Gabriel told Mary: "*The Holy Ghost shall come upon you, and the power of the Highest shall overshadow you; therefore, that holy thing which shall be born of you shall be (future tense) called the Son of God.*"

The same construction is used by the writer to the Hebrews, here in verse 5. "*I WILL BE a father to Him, and He SHALL BE my Son.*" It seems reasonable to suppose that God would not speak of something as being in the future if it had been a fact for all eternity. It makes more sense to conclude that the Father/Son relationship was going to be between the man, Jesus, and the Godhead. That is why Adam is referred to as being "*the first man*" (not only in time but also in relationship) and Christ is referred to as "*the second man, the Lord from heaven.*"

Obviously, Jesus was not the second man to be born. Many men lived between Adam and Christ, but only two enjoyed an intimate, sinless relationship with the Almighty. The first man (Adam) blew it. He sinned. The wonderful relationship he had enjoyed with his Maker was ruined, and the whole human race was plunged into the grip of sin and death. The second man (Jesus) saw it through, maintained the spotless relationship to the end, and carried it out into eternity unbroken. He did it on our behalf.

Verse 6:

"But again, when He brought the firstborn into the world, He says: "Let all the angels of God worship Him."

The greater being can never worship the lesser. When John was confronted by an angel, in Revelation 19:10, he fell at his fee to worship him, but the angel said, *"Don't do it, for I am your fellow-servant, and of your brethren that have the testimony of Jesus. Worship God!"* The angel would not accept worship because he was a created being. The same thing happened again in Revelation 22:9, and again the angel refused to accept worship. He said, in effect, *"Don't worship me, worship God!"* In Colossians 2:18, Paul warns his readers: *"Let no man rob you of your reward, in false humility and the worshipping of angels."* Satan would love to see that. He was originally an angel, and desires more than anything else to be worshipped. He told Jesus, *"All these* (the kingdoms of the earth) *will I give you, if you will fall down and worship me."*

In Revelation 5 we find a different picture. There, John recounts the scene that unfolded around the throne of the universe:

"I beheld, and I heard the voice of many angels around the throne, and the living creatures, and the elders. The number of them was ten thousand times ten thousand, and thousands of thousands, saying with a loud voice, Worthy is the Lamb that was slain to receive power, and riches, and wisdom, and strength, and honor and glory and blessing, And every creature which is in heaven, and on earth, and under the earth, and such as are in the sea, and all that are in them, heard I saying: Blessing, and honor and glory and power, be unto Him who sits upon the throne, and unto the Lamb,

forever and ever. And the four living creatures said, Amen. And the four and twenty elders fell down and worshipped Him that lives forever and ever."

The Lamb, of course, is the Lord Jesus, and He accepts the worship of His creatures, because He is God.

Verse 7:

"And of the angels He says: "Who makes His angels spirits and His ministers a flame of fire."

The Son is identified specifically as God. His throne is identified as "eternal". His character is identified as "righteous". He is the only begotten Son of God, who is a man, and in Him humanity has been elevated to the very throne of glory! I often wonder how those who insist that Jesus was nothing but a great teacher, or a prophet, or an angel, interpret these verses. They must close their eyes and ears to them. They do not want to acknowledge that Jesus, the Maker, Controller and Judge of all the universe is to be worshipped. "Jesus, the teacher" or "Jesus the angel" is far easier for them to accept because in those roles He does not demand submission. A teacher can be questioned or debated but the Lord of all the universe does not offer that option.

For centuries, people have done their best to discredit the Bible. The reason for this is simple. If the Bible is true, then what it says must be accepted, and what it says is distasteful to the natural man. The Bible calls man a sinner and tells him he is heading for judgment. It tells him that he is incapable of helping himself and warns him that if he wishes to avoid perdition he must surrender to Christ. These truths wound man's ego; they strike at the heart of his pride. Consequently, he resists them and, since attack is often the best form of defense, he seeks to prove that the Bible is false – nothing but legend and fable. He searches for contradictions, which he feels will weaken the Bible's credibility. Unfortunately for him, *"the natural man receives not the things of the Spirit; they are foolishness to him. Neither can he know them, for they are spiritually discerned."* The unsaved man sees only the surface facts. He does not comprehend the spiritual significance of what he reads. His "wisdom" becomes foolishness before God.

Verse 8:

"But to the Son He says: Your throne, O God, is forever and ever; a scepter of righteousness is the scepter of Your Kingdom."

Nothing could be clearer than that statement. It identifies the Son (Christ) as God. His throne is forever and ever, and His kingdom is ruled in righteousness. However, the next verse (verse 9) is taken by some as a contradiction:

"You have loved righteousness and hated lawlessness; therefore God, Your God, has anointed You with the oil of gladness more than Your companions (fellows)."

Here the Son is seen to have received an anointing from God, and is identified with others, who are termed *"companions"*, or *"fellows."* The question naturally arises, "How could the same person be supreme in verse 8 and subordinate in verse 9?" This is typical of the verses that are seized upon by those who search for inaccuracies in the Scriptures and attempt to discredit the divinity of Jesus Christ. Thus, it is important for us to find a satisfactory explanation from Scripture itself. Two main Scriptures are sufficient to provide us with direction, both of which are well-known to us. The first is John 1:1-3;

'In the beginning was the Word, and the Word was with God, and the Word was God. The same was in the beginning with God. All things were made by Him and without Him was not anything made that was made."

This establishes, beyond doubt, that *"the Word"* and God were one and the same. Referring to *"the Word"* as *"Him"* clarifies that He was not simply an inanimate force but a Person. Only God could create from nothing, and the Word is seen here to be the creator of all things. Then, in verse 14 of the same chapter, we read: *"And the Word became flesh and dwelt among us."* There is no way round that verse either. The Creator God, who always existed in eternity, became flesh in time and dwelt among men, without losing His divinity. Jesus was able to say, in John 3:13: *"No man has ascended **up** into heaven, but He who came **down** from heaven, even the Son of Man, who is **in** heaven."* That statement is difficult for us to grasp. We are working at a disadvantage, since we don't even know where heaven is! Just before His death, Jesus prayed: "*Now, O Father, glorify me with your own self, with the glory that I had with you before the world was.*" He was about to return to the glory in which He had always existed before His entrance into the world of men.

The second Scripture is Philippians 2:5-7:

"*Let this mind be in you, which was also in Christ Jesus. Who, being in the form of God, thought it not an object of desire to be equal with God.*"

The word translated "*form*" does not indicate an outward resemblance, as if somebody dressed up to look like another. It describes the actual outward expression of the inner substance. In other words, Jesus could only have been in the "form" of God by actually *being* God.

The passage continues:

"*But made Himself of no reputation and took upon Himself the "form" of a servant, and was made in the likeness of men.*"

The same word "*form*" (morphe) is used again, meaning that just as in eternity past Jesus was God in every sense of the word, so, in time, He took upon Himself the actual "form" (identity) of a servant. He was as really a servant as He was really God, and as a servant, He "*became obedient.*" There is the key, and there is the marvel. The creator became obedient in order that disobedient men and women might be saved from their own sin. Obedience brought us salvation. As Paul wrote in Romans 5:19: "*For as by one man's disobedience many were made sinners, so by the obedience of one shall many be made righteous.*"

To sum up, The Word, who was God, became a man and God spoke to us through Him. In His capacity as God, He was co-equal with the Godhead. In His capacity as perfect man, He looked to the Father as His God and was obedient to Him. In His capacity as Mediator, Jesus represented mankind before God and God dealt with His Son in that capacity. Jesus was a man in every respect. He experienced pain, sorrow, joy, hunger and thirst. Everything He did during His 33 years on the earth, He did on behalf of the human race. He accomplished, as a man, all that the human race had failed to accomplish. He became the bridge across the gulf which had opened up between God and man as the result of man's sin. This mediatorial role will continue for all eternity. Thus, as God who became flesh, He was anointed with the oil of gladness, far above that of all men and angels.

Christ is eternal

Verses 10-12:

"And: "You, Lord, in the beginning laid the foundation of the earth, and the heavens are the work of Your hands; 11 They will perish, but You remain; and they will all grow old like a garment; 12 Like a cloak You will fold them up, and they will be changed. But You are the same, and Your years will not fail."

From Christ's perfect humanity we now look back to His perfect divinity. To introduce us to the Lord's relationship with the created universe, in which He temporarily lived, the writer quotes Psalm 102:25-27. Long before Jesus was born, the Psalmist was speaking of the pre-incarnate Christ. Notice the five points the writer makes:

1. **The stellar heavens were created by Him**. As we have seen, the man, Jesus, did not create the heavens, but the Word who became Jesus created them.

2. **They shall perish**. A time limit has been placed on their existence. There will come a time when they cease to exist. Peter refers to that time in his second letter. He writes:

"But the day of the Lord will come as a thief in the night, at which time the heavens shall pass away with a great noise, and the elements shall melt with a fervent heat. The earth also, and the works that are therein, shall be burned up."

This does not mean that this terrible cataclysm might suddenly take place while we live on the earth. God will preserve the earth until His program is completed. It will take place after the millennium and after the final judgment (Revelation 21:1).

3. **They will grow old like a garment** (the physical universe will wear out). Everything finite wears out in the end, and the earth

is already giving signals that such a condition is approaching. There are water shortages all over the globe; earthquakes and eruptions speak of instability. In God's economy, nothing of this magnitude happens overnight. But signs are beginning to increase, indicating that the final days are approaching.

4. **The heavens will be folded up and changed**. John wrote in Revelation 21:11: *"I saw a new Heaven and a new earth, for the first heaven and the first earth were passed away."* Mankind looks upon the physical universe as the epitome of stability, reliability and security. Yet it is destined to be folded up and replaced by the Creator. The truth is that the present universe is temporary, insecure, unstable and unreliable. The earth upon which we stand, the sun that warms us and gives us light, and the myriad stars in the sky, all have an assigned limit. Where, then, can we turn for the stability and security we desire?

5. **Christ will remain**. He will never change. He is eternal. When everything we now know has been removed, He will still be there. What more do we need? Jesus said: *"Heaven and earth shall pass away, but my word will not pass away."* Bibles will pass away. When the heavens are burned up with a fervent heat, not one Bible will be left. But God's Word will remain. The Word of God is the will of God, the truth of God, the promises of God. These eternal things do not rely upon paper and ink for their survival. God's Word instructs us and warns us; it gives us His promises, but the promises themselves are intangible. The Bible cannot fulfill one promise. Nor can it save one soul. Only God's Spirit can bring those things to pass. Our hope and security must be in Him.

Verse 13:

"But to which of the angels has He ever said: "Sit at My right hand, Till I make Your enemies Your footstool"?

Obviously, God never said that to any angel, but He did say it to the Lord Jesus. Here the writer is quoting from Psalm 110. Angels stand before the throne, or bow before it. Jesus sat down upon it, taking His place as co-ruler. He is invited to sit at the Father's right hand until His enemies prostrate themselves at His feet.

Verse 14:

"Are they not all ministering spirits sent forth to minister for those who will inherit salvation?"

There are no exceptions. All angels are messengers of God. They never reign; their role is to serve. They are "sent forth" by God to minister to (serve) those who will inherit salvation. They minister but do not preach. Peter stated that the angels desire to look into the subject of salvation. Apparently they do not fully understand it but are curious to know more. God sends them out to watch over you and me, though we are seldom conscious of their presence. They protect and guide in ways unseen, yet, despite their invisibility, they are present with us all the time. Nevertheless, our trust must never be placed in angels. It must be in the Lord Jesus, the One whose perfect will the angels obey.

CHAPTER 2

The establishment of Christ's supremacy in chapter 1 has a purpose beyond that of confirming the fact itself. What follows in chapter 2 is based upon it and grows out of it. The writer is saying that we must have a clear picture of who Jesus is before we can grasp the significance of what follows.

Give heed to Christ's word

Verse 1:

"*Therefore. . . .*"

The word "*therefore*" introduces a conclusion, based upon the contents of the previous section. "Because of the truths we have considered in chapter 1"-

"*Therefore we must give the more earnest heed to the things we have heard, lest we drift away.*"

The Authorized Version has "*ought* to give heed" but the sense is stronger than that. It is imperative, which makes taking heed a necessity. Since God has spoken to us through His Son, it would be the height of folly to disregard what He has said. By failing to take heed, we are in danger of "drifting by". The *words* will not drift by. They will remain, like rocks in a river, whether we listen to them or not. The risk lies in the fact that *we* might drift by the words. It is possible to sit in church, week by week, but allow the teaching of God's Word to go over our heads. Under those circumstances, we are no better off than if we had never attended the services. There was an extreme case, one Easter Sunday morning, when a man in the congregation was seen watching a ball game on his i-phone during the message. He certainly "drifted by" whatever was said that day. Most people are not quite as obvious as that, but they still allow their thoughts to wander.

Jesus touched on the same idea in His parable of the Sower and the Soils. He said that some seed never even germinates because the birds come and snatch it away as soon as it is sown. We must not allow the enemy to dull our senses and render us impervious to the good seed of God's Word. Based upon who Jesus is (chapter1) it is essential that we give "the more earnest heed" to what He has to say. The reason why it is essential is spelled out in the next two verses.

Verses 2-3:

"For if the word spoken through angels proved steadfast, and every transgression and disobedience received a just reward, 3 how shall we escape if we neglect so great a salvation, which at the first began to be spoken by the Lord, and was confirmed to us by those who heard Him?"

It is essential that we grasp the significance of that question. What was the word spoken by angels? It was the law which God gave to Israel through Moses. We naturally have a picture in our minds of Moses going up into the mountain and receiving the law directly from God, and there is truth in that picture. However, other Scriptures suggest a different scenario. In Acts 7:53, for instance, Stephen accused the religious rulers of *"receiving the law by the dispensation of angels"* and not keeping it. Paul, in Galatians 3:19 claimed that the law was *"ordained by angels."* Undoubtedly, the Law was God's creation, and it is equally certain that God Himself was on the mountain with Moses. That is why Moses was placed in a cleft of the rock and allowed to see only a partial view of God (Exodus 33:22), returning to his people with a face so radiant that he had to veil it from them. However, angels were evidently used as instruments in some way, in bringing the law to Israel.

Here, in verse 2, we are reminded that the law was strictly enforced, so that *"every transgression and disobedience received a just reward."* Hebrews 10:28 says: *"He who despised Moses' law died without mercy under two or three witnesses."* This, in turn, was a reference to Deuteronomy 17:2 and 6. In other words, the law was to be taken very seriously.

Now, in these last days, God has given us a new covenant, superior to the old. He has spoken to us, not through angels but through His Son. In view of such an astounding privilege, the writer to the Hebrews asks (verse 3), "*How shall we escape if we neglect so great a salvation, which at the first began to be spoken by the Lord, and was confirmed to us by those who heard Him?*" The "*so great salvation*" was promised in the Old Testament and then proclaimed in the New, first by Jesus Himself, then by the apostles, who participated in the great events of Acts chapter 2, and later still by Paul, who described himself as "*an apostle born out of time.*"

Three questions arise from this paragraph. **First, what does the word "*neglect*" mean?** The word translated "neglect" literally means, "*to make light of,*" to treat as if it were of no importance. There are a great many people today who dismiss the subject of salvation as if it were of no importance. Education, money, and football are considered to be important, but salvation is shrugged off as something only religious people contemplate. Unfortunately, religious people are not the only ones who die. Everyone has to die sooner or later. Then salvation takes on a whole new meaning. By that time it is too late to do anything about it. The present generation sits in front of the television for hours at a time, watching people die in a variety of ways, without ever asking if they are ready to follow the same route. So "neglect", in this sense, is not rejection. It is simply a blind disregard for the gift of forgiveness and eternal life.

Second, who does the writer mean by "we"? (*How shall we escape?*) Does he include himself, or is he simply using the "*we*" to soften the impact on his readers? Obviously the writer of this letter was a true Christian, writing to Christians. Some were experiencing difficulties but they were nevertheless genuinely saved. Others who read the letter were probably seeking but not yet fully persuaded, and still others had never made a profession at all. Obviously a cross section of people read these words and reacted in a variety of ways, just as they still do today. The "*we*", therefore, refers to anyone who reads the letter, regardless of his or her stage of spiritual maturity. Anyone, Christian and non-Christian alike could "*neglect*" or disregard God's Word and the result would be different in each case.

Third, what would we escape from? The writer doesn't tell us. He leaves us to fill in the blanks for ourselves. I suspect the reason is that what we escape from depends on where we stand, personally. It is possible for a genuine Christian to "drift by" the Word of God and thus gain no benefit from its teaching. It is also possible for a genuine Christian to "neglect" the great salvation which he already possesses, and which will never be taken from him. Nevertheless, both sins will result in loss. He will not lose his salvation because that is based squarely upon the achievements and merits of Christ, but at the judgment seat of Christ, where our service will be evaluated, we shall not be able to escape loss (1 Corinthians 3:11-15). There is also the loss of present joy and assurance, which is forfeited by apathy and neglect. More serious yet is the position of those who have never received Christ as their savior. The Bible says that they are lost without hope, without God in this world, and look forward to only eternal darkness.

The writer makes no statement. He does not say, *"We shall not escape!"* Instead, he asks a question, *"How shall we escape?"* and leaves us to answer it. How do we plan to avoid the inevitable confrontation with Christ? Not all things are within our grasp. For instance, we do not decide when we shall die, but we do decide how we shall live and how much effort we invest in our walk with Christ. At the bema seat, the Christian's service will be evaluated, rewards will be received and lost, but salvation is guaranteed. Those who have never trusted Christ will not appear on that day, but will stand before the great white throne at the end of the age, by which time the opportunity to receive Christ will have passed. In Revelation 20:11-15, John wrote:

> *"I saw the dead, small and great, stand before God; and the books were opened; and another book was opened, which is the book of life: and the dead were judged out of those things which were written in the books, according to their works . . .and whosoever was not found written in the book of life was cast into the lake of fire."*

The question remains, *"How shall we escape if we neglect so great salvation?"* The answer is that there is no escape. It behooves us all to take God's Word seriously, whether we are saved or unsaved, because neglecting it brings inevitable and clearly prescribed consequences.

Verse 4:

"God also bearing witness both with signs and wonders, with various miracles, and gifts of the Holy Spirit, according to His own will."

This verse forms a continuation of verse 3. It describes the *"great salvation, which at the first began to be spoken by the Lord, and was confirmed to us by those who heard Him."* Jesus spoke of it first to the apostles, who proclaimed the good news at Pentecost and beyond. The book of Acts contains many accounts of how God wrought signs and wonders in those early days to confirm the authenticity of the Gospel. Many sick folk were healed, sinners were struck down, prisons were opened and the ground shaken. Some were even brought back from the dead. Those were the exceptions, but a constant throughout the church age has been the distribution of spiritual gifts to all believers, so that the church has grown as a living organism. All these marvels of confirmation are the direct work of God. Angels have been involved rarely, and then only as messengers.

In proving that Christ is superior in every way to the angels, the writer to the Hebrews had to overcome an important obstacle. *"How can this man, Jesus, be superior to the angels, seeing that He died, while angels are immortal?"* This was a real stumbling block to the Jews. The cross was an offense to them. It was difficult to accept, difficult to get around. It is still difficult today. Sooner or later all those who search for the truth must come face to face with the cross. It is unavoidable. Paul wrote: *"The message of the cross is to those who are perishing, foolishness, but to those who are saved it is the power of God."* (1 Corinthians 1:18). Why should this be? Why should a common instrument of execution become the focus of such contention, and over such a long period of time? The answer depends on our view of the man, Jesus. It is not the cross that matters, but what we understand was accomplished on it.

Those who look upon Jesus as simply "a great teacher" or "a great prophet" see in His death nothing but a tragic end to a promising career. To follow a man who was executed as a criminal for offending the Pharisees would be foolishness. However, if we view Jesus as being who He claimed to be (and all the evidence confirms that He was) then the cross takes on a whole new meaning. In the first view, Jesus was arrested by a superior authority, and put to death against His will for being a nuisance; in the second view He was the creator and controller of the universe, who voluntarily became a man and then willingly laid down His life in order to carry through His plan. The purpose of His incarnation was to paralyze forever the power of Satan over the souls of men. Those who hold to the first view are perishing because they do not believe; those who subscribe to the second recognize the cross as the symbol of their salvation.

Clearly, the physical cross is of no spiritual value. Major Ian Thomas, the founder of the worldwide Capernwray Bible Schools, took exception to the hymn, "The Old Rugged Cross", because he felt it tends to romanticize the physical object. There was nothing beautiful about the cross. It was a diabolical instrument of torture that symbolized the lowest form of human moral degradation. By contrast, the victory that was won upon it was earth-shattering in its implications.

The wonder of the incarnation

In the next section, the writer to the Hebrews seeks to demonstrate the fathomless truth behind the incarnation and death of Jesus.

Verses 5-8a:

"For He has not put the world to come, of which we speak, in subjection to angels. 6 But one testified in a certain place, saying: "What is man that You are mindful of him, or the son of man that You take care of him? 7 You made him a little lower than the angels; You crowned him with glory and honor, and set him over the works of Your hands. 8 You have put all things in subjection under his feet."

The *"one"* in verse 6 who *"testified in a certain place"* was David, and the *"certain place"* was Psalm 8. Verses 6-8 are a quotation from that Psalm. The Hebrews accepted David as one who had divine authority. Who did God make *"a little lower than the angels?"* Who did He *"set over the works of His hands?"* Dr. Wuest points out that in this particular passage both the Old Testament Hebrew and the New Testament Greek make it clear that the human race is in view, personified by Adam, its federal head. God did crown Adam with glory and honor and all things were placed in subjection to him. But then Adam sinned and forfeited his position. He remained dominant over nature, but instead of the original domination, which was based upon trust, his new domination was based upon fear. Originally the animals came to Adam to be named. There was no danger then; they were not afraid of him. They did not know what danger or fear were. Now everything has changed. The birds keep their distance and the animals run away (with very good reason) because man has become a destroyer. Adam's kingdom was cursed because of sin. Some of the beauty remained, as we see all around us today, but lurking behind the beauty are pain and misery. Thorns, weeds and disease took over, earthquakes, tornadoes, hurricanes, floods, famines and plagues cause all nature to struggle for survival. Back of all that, death began to reign on the earth. It became the unavoidable nemesis, which eventually claims all living things. Worst of all, Satan took over as *"the god of this world."* But (thankfully) only for a limited time.

Man was made *"a little lower than the angels"* for a fixed period of time. The length of this period is decided by God. The boundaries have already been fixed. They were decided before the universe was created but have not yet been revealed. This is the sense of the remainder of verse 8:

> *"In putting everything under him, God left nothing that is not subject to him. Yet at present we not see everything subject to him."* (NIV)

The subjection of the earth to Adam was absolute. Nothing was excluded (Genesis 1:28-30). But as we look around today it is easy to see that there are many things that are no longer under man's control. The dwindling resources of the earth, for instance, and the natural disasters which man is unable to predict or prevent, are examples of his impotence. Outside God's intervention there is little hope for the human race. Not only is man unable to control climatic and geophysical conditions but he cannot even to control himself! He tries but he fails. On the domestic front, there is a growing sense of despair, as violence increases and families break apart. People are discovering that despite a proliferation of gadgets and conveniences, which should make life more satisfying, the sinfulness of man undermines everything else. The same is true of the political scene, both national and international. Outside God, there is no control. At home, politicians fight endlessly, producing no real solutions, while in the world at large, nation rises against nation and kingdom against kingdom. There are wars and rumors of wars, because one section of humanity wants to control other sections, even though they are unable to control themselves! The peaceful domination given to man by God in the garden was lost because of sin. But thankfully, that is not the end of the story.

Christ's vicarious suffering

Verse 9:

> *"But we see Jesus, who was made a little lower than the angels, for the suffering of death, crowned with glory and honor, that He, by the grace of God, might taste death for everyone."*

By becoming a man, the second Person of the Trinity allowed Himself to become *"lower than the angels"* for just a brief period of time. His purpose in doing so was *"that He might taste death for everyone."* God could not taste death, nor could the angels. Only by entering the human race could He experience the common sentence passed upon all flesh as the result of sin. It was a deliberate subjection, a deliberate submission to the one thing that held the human race in a vice-grip. He deliberately allowed Himself to be "made sin" (2 Corinthians 5:21) and die as the representative of all men, in order that He might break death's grip, once for all. Paul described this clearly in his letter to the Philippians:

> *". . being in the form of God, did not consider it robbery to be equal with God, 7 but made Himself of no reputation, taking the form of a bond-servant, and coming in the likeness of men. 8 And being found in appearance as a man, He humbled Himself and became obedient to the point of death, even the death of the cross. 9 Therefore also God has highly exalted Him and given Him a name which is above every name, 10 that at the name of Jesus every knee shall bow, of those in Heaven and of those on earth, and of those under the earth, 11 and that every tongue should confess that Jesus Christ is Lord, to the glory of God the Father."* (Philippians 2:6-11)

This same Jesus, who humbled Himself for the sake of us all is now *"crowned with glory and honor."* One day He will return to reign and all believers will return with Him. Though, at present, they are "lower than the angels", one day they will be exalted above them and be privileged to reign with Christ. 1 Corinthians 6:3 says: *"Do you not know that we shall judge angels?"* Revelation 20:6 says:

> *"Blessed and holy is he who has part in the first resurrection . . . . they shall be priests of God and of Christ, and shall reign with Him for a thousand years."*

The passage has not finished with the subject. Continuing to demonstrate Christ's incarnation and sufferings, verse 10 continues:

> *"For it was fitting for Him, for whom are all things and by whom are all things, in bringing many sons to glory, to make the author of their salvation perfect through sufferings."*

Here is a concept which is not easy to grasp. The Word, who became Jesus, was God. Obviously, God is by nature perfect in all His ways. Had the Lord not been perfect, He could not have atoned for the sin of mankind. So how could He have been *"made perfect"* through suffering? The answer lies in two areas: first, in Christ's humanity, and second, in the meaning of the word translated *"perfect."* The humanity of Jesus was detailed in verse 9. His suffering and death achieved something unachievable any other way. It brought to completion the total identification of Christ with the human race. That is the meaning of the word translated *"perfect"* in our English Bibles. Christ's human experience found completion in His death.

The Word did not become a man for His own benefit or amusement. Everything He did was carried out in a substitutionary capacity and the benefit was credited to us. *"He was wounded for our transgressions; He was bruised for our iniquities; the chastisement of our peace was upon Him and with His stripes we are healed."* (Isaiah 53:5). He experienced the whole gamut of human emotions – hunger, thirst, pain, grief, sorrow, temptation, injustice and rejection. Finally, He died, and with His death, His human experience was completed (perfected). His identification with His creation was so complete that afterwards He was able to refer to believers as "His brethren." This is explained in the next verses.

Identification with Christ

Verses 11-13:

"For both He who sanctifies and those who are being sanctified are all of one, for which reason He is not ashamed to call them brethren, 12 saying: "I will declare Your name to My brethren; in the midst of the assembly I will sing praise to You. 13 And again: "I will put My trust in Him." And again: "Here am I and the children whom God has given Me."

"To sanctify" means *"to make holy"*, *"to set apart."* Jesus won sanctification by His death and we received the benefit. Therefore we are one with Him and on that basis He recognizes us as *"brethren."* This does not suggest that He stooped low in order to call us brethren. It means that He raised us up so high that He was able to identify us with Him without forfeiting His perfection! By recognizing us as His brethren, He demonstrates the absolute nature of His victory over sin.

Verses 12-13 contain three quotations from the Old Testament. The first comes from Psalm 22:22 while the second and third are taken from Isaiah 8:17-18. We should bear in mind that the original readers of this letter did not have the New Testament for reference. The writer therefore used the Old Testament Scriptures to support his statements. Man has no authority outside the Scriptures and it is important to base our belief system on what the Bible says. The remainder of the chapter continues to explain the purpose of Christ's suffering and death.

Verses 14-15:

"Inasmuch then as the children have partaken of flesh and blood, He Himself likewise shared in the same, that through death He might destroy him who had the power of death, that is, the devil, 15 and release those who through fear of death were all their lifetime subject to bondage."

Here are three plain truths. Truth #1: Christ became a man; He became a *"partaker of flesh and blood"* just like us. Truth #2: The devil's power was destroyed by Christ's death. Truth #3: Mankind, who was under the sentence of death, was released from bondage. The first truth is easy to grasp and needs no explanation. The second truth is not quite so simple. How was the devil's power broken by Christ's death? And if it was broken how come Satan is still so active today? Of course God, not Satan, has the power of physical death. Psalm 68:20 says, "*Unto God the Lord, belong the issues of life.*" And 1 Samuel 2:6 says "*The Lord kills and makes alive. He brings down to the grave and brings up.*" We are not thinking of physical death here. We are thinking of spiritual death.

When God placed Adam in the Garden of Eden, He warned him not to eat from the tree of the knowledge of good and evil. He said, "*In the day that you eat of it you shall surely die.*" He was not referring to physical death. Adam lived for many years after he disobeyed God's command, but he died spiritually. His sin cut him off from fellowship with God. Satan knew this would be the consequence of disobedience, and managed to deceive Adam and Eve into breaking God's command. It was a deliberate strategy. He calculated that the first parents could not pass on spiritual life to their heirs if they no longer possessed it themselves. Thus the whole future human race would be born into spiritual death and Satan would hold the master card. He calculated that a holy God could not allow fallen men and women into His presence and that God's own perfection would be the barrier that would cut men and women off from His presence. Man's sin and God's righteousness together would guarantee Satan's power over all humanity. Satan could claim that because man was a sinner, God was bound to cut him off. His plan worked, and the very first child to be born into this world (Cain) grew up to be a murderer!

The situation seemed irremediable. Man was incapable of regaining the standard of righteousness necessary to bridge the gap back into fellowship with God, and despite His love, God could not reach back to man without violating His own perfection. Death reigned and man was in bondage to it. But God had a master plan. Suppose He broke the cycle of sin by coming into the world *Himself*, not as a descendant of Adam but as a new creation through a virgin birth! Suppose He grew up normally as a member of the human race, yet free from the sin nature inherent in everyone else? Under those circumstances He would be immune from the curse placed upon the rest of humanity and therefore not subject to death. But suppose, as the only perfect

man, He voluntarily laid down His life and accepted in His own being
the penalty of spiritual death, which hung over all mankind? And then
suppose that, having died, He was raised to life again, as proof that the
price had been paid and the account forever settled? Satan's master card
would be immediately invalidated and his power over the human race
neutralized! As we know, God's plan was carried out and the human
race was delivered

This, of course, did not guarantee universal salvation. Some preach that
it does, but Scripture teaches otherwise. It is true that we could walk up
to anyone in the street and say with absolute confidence, *"Your sins have
been paid for."* This is a fact that applies to every individual alive. All
men and women are potentially saved but, as with all free gifts, salvation
has to be received before it becomes a personal fact. Salvation cannot
be seen or touched, and it must be received by faith, based upon the
promises of Scripture. *"Without faith, it is impossible to please God, but
he who comes to Him must believe that He is, and that He is a rewarder of
those who diligently seek Him."* (Hebrews 11:6).

The seed of Abraham

Verse 16:

*"For indeed He does not give aid to angels, but He does give aid to
the seed of Abraham."*

The King James Bible translates *"give aid"* as *"took on Him the nature
of."* The term means *"to lay hold of"* and was interpreted more or less
literally by the Authorized translators. Today, the sense of *"giving aid"* is
almost universally embraced. The ministry of Jesus was not designed to
help angels. They did not descend from Adam and therefore they were
not candidates for salvation. There is no salvation for the angels who
rebelled. Instead, Jesus came to seek and to save *"the seed of Abraham."*
By this we immediately think of the Jews – and certainly Jews were
included in the offer of redemption. All the original disciples were Jews
and many in the first crowds to be saved, both before and after Pentecost,
were Jews. But Paul was sent to preach the Gospel to Gentiles and in
Galatians 3:29 he wrote: *"If you are Christ's, then you are Abraham's seed,*

and heirs according to the promise." In fact, a careful reading of Galatians 3:15-29 is very profitable.

Finally in this chapter, Verses 17-18:

> "*Therefore, in all things He had to be made like His brethren, that He might be a merciful and faithful High Priest in things pertaining to God, to make propitiation for the sins of the people. 18 For in that He Himself has suffered, being tempted, He is able to aid those who are tempted.*"

As we established previously, the eternal Word had to become a man in order to represent mankind before the throne of God. He had to be "*made like His brethren*" in every respect except for sin. In chapter 5 of this letter the High Priesthood of Jesus will be discussed at length. The Jewish High Priest was appointed to "*make propitiation*" for the sins of the people by sprinkling the blood of the sacrifice on the mercy seat (which represented God's throne). Jesus offered up His own blood as an atonement for the sins of all mankind.

We are told that Jesus was "*tested on all points as we are, yet without sin.*"(Hebrews 4:15) .That being so, there is no problem that can assail us that He has not experienced and cannot therefore understand what we are going through. He knows because He has been there, not as an angel or some mysterious spirit, but as a man of flesh and blood, conscious of emotion and pain. We have a God in Heaven who remembers what it is like to suffer!

CHAPTER 3

Christ the High Priest

Verse 1:

"Therefore, holy brethren, partakers of the heavenly calling, consider the Apostle and High Priest of our confession, Christ Jesus."

Two words are used in this verse which require clarification. The first is "*holy*" and the second is "*calling*". Both have an important bearing on the way we should live. We saw in the previous chapter that the atonement won for us by Christ was so complete that He is free to call us "*brethren*" without violating His perfect righteousness. Brethren, of course, are the sons of the same father, and sharers of the same life. And since the Father of the Lord Jesus is God Himself, we are considered children of God by the authority of God's Word.

However, Christians are not merely "brethren;" they are "*holy*" brethren, which means that God has set them apart for His own use. This immediately raises one of those awkward questions which we need to ask from time to time, namely, "If all Christians are holy, why do some of them live such unholy lives?" There seem to be only two possible solutions to this question. Either they are not brethren at all, or they are children of the light who, for some reason, prefer to walk in darkness. The world is quick to point them out as evidence to support its claim that the Christian faith is phony. The media delight in showcasing church-goers who get involved in immoral or illegal practices. The deeper they are associated with a church, the better reporters like it. The inference is fed to the public that Christianity is merely a cloak under which evil people hide. Sadly, this is sometimes true. Professing Christians do occasionally bring reproach upon the name of Christ. Whether or not their profession is genuine is for God to judge, but certainly their behavior brings the genuineness of their faith into question. Criminal actions by professing Christians are rare, but errant social behavior is far more common. For instance, the language some of them use on the job during the week belies their pious manner in church on Sunday. The way some conduct business also brings doubt upon their profession. Similarly, the manner in which some professing Christians treat their spouses brings discredit to their faith. The worlds look at the church and points out the hypocrites as reasons why they want nothing to do with Christianity. We all know that that argument is hollow, and we also know that the counterfeit simply proves the existence of the true, but that does not alter the fact that the behavior of some provides ammunition to those who are looking for something to criticize.

Holiness, of course, is not something which we achieve. It is a free gift which we are given. Christians are *decreed* to be holy by God. We were bought with a price and are therefore not our own. We are set apart to serve and it is sad when a "holy" person engages in unholy pursuits. It spits in God's face and scorns the suffering of Christ. It is important that we take stock of our lives and insure that we are not falling below the standard God demands. At the same time, we should remember that holiness is not the same as gloominess. We can still laugh and have fun. Man did not invent humor, God did. We would not know what "funny" was if God had not built a sense of humor into us. Being holy involves remembering who we are and whom we serve. It involves living with eternity in view and avoiding those things which night ensnare us.

There is a popular saying which claims that we can be "*so heavenly minded that we are no earthly good.*" That is a cute saying but it is also complete rubbish. Jesus was more heavenly minded than any of us, but we could hardly accuse Him of being "*no earthly good*". Today, a more accurate statement would seem to be that some Christians are "*so earthly minded that they are no heavenly good.*" That is a far more serious problem.

So much, then for the first word ("*holy*"). The second important word in this verse is "*calling*". ("*Wherefore, holy brethren, partakers of the heavenly calling. . .*") The Scriptures are peppered with references to the

Christian's calling. Even the word "church", which is so familiar to us, means *"called out ones."* Every one of us was chosen and called by God. Had He not taken the initiative, we would never have known Him. Jesus said, *"You have not chosen me but I have chosen you."* He called us, personally, into fellowship with Himself, just as He did His disciples. Now He expects us to respond. Ephesians 4:1 says: *"I beseech you that you walk worthy of the calling with which you are called."* The notion of receiving Christ and then continuing on as we were before we were saved is completely contrary to the Word of God. Paul told the Corinthians, *"If any man be in Christ, he is a new creation. Old things have passed away, behold, all things have become new."* This is not a command but a statement of fact. It is the inevitable result of the calling. So where do we look for direction? The answer is in verse 1 again:

> *"Therefore, holy brethren, partakers of the heavenly calling, consider the Apostle and High Priest of our confession, Christ Jesus. "*

The word *"consider"* means literally *"to ponder thoroughly in one's mind"* -- *"to think something through."* In this case, we are to ponder on *"the apostle and high priest of our confession, Christ Jesus."* Here lies the secret of a holy life. We are to keep our eyes on Him. *"Looking unto Jesus, the author and finisher of faith."* He is to be the focal point of our lives. Greater than the prophets, mightier than the angels, He is the "Apostle" of our confession. An apostle is "one sent" and Jesus was sent from God to rescue a lost race from destruction. In that capacity, He was the originator of our faith. We might say He invented the very concept of salvation. But there is more. Because Jesus now represents us before the throne of the universe and intercedes on our behalf, He is also the high priest of our confession. We shall examine this in greater detail when we get to chapter 5.

Verses 2-6a:

> *"Who was faithful to Him who appointed Him, as Moses also was faithful in all His house. 3 For this One has been counted worthy of more glory than Moses, inasmuch as He who built the house has more honor than the house. 4 For every house is built by someone, but He who built all things is God. 5 And Moses indeed was faithful in all His house as a servant, for a testimony of those*

things which would be spoken afterward, 6 but Christ as a Son over His own house. . ."

The word "*house*", here, refers to a family. The queen of England belongs to the "House of Windsor"; Moses was faithful over the "House of Israel." He forfeited the treasures of Egypt in order to remain faithful to it. Materially and socially, it cost him everything he had, but he was willing to suffer reproach rather than betray his call. Jesus also was faithful, but to a different house. He left the glory of His Father's throne and willingly suffered affliction in order to carry out God's will. The difference was that Moses was faithful as a servant over people belonging to another Head, while Christ was the creator of everything, and came as a Son over His own inheritance. That brings us to the end of verse 6:

"Whose house we are if we hold fast the confidence and the rejoicing of the hope firm to the end."

We (all Christians) are the "*house*" over which Christ came to reign. At first glance this verse looks suspiciously like a condition. "*We are His house IF. . .*" It seems to say that we will be Christ's house provided we manage to maintain the required standard all the way to the end. If this were so, then the reverse would also have to be true, namely, if we failed to make the grade from now to the end we would cease to be His house, and would therefore lose our salvation! That, of course, could never happen. Paul told the Philippians that having begun a good work in a believer, God will perform it until the day of Jesus Christ. He wrote to the Ephesians that Christians are sealed with the Holy Spirit of Promise, who is the guarantee of their inheritance until the redemption of the purchased possession, Peter wrote that believers are kept by the power of God unto salvation, and Jesus Himself stated that His sheep will never perish and nothing could pluck them out of His hand. How then will we interpret verse 6b?

The answer lies in the word "*if.*" There are three Greek words translated "*if*" in our English language, and they all mean different things. One means "*if, and it's true*", another means "*if, and it's not true*" and the third means "*if, maybe it's true, maybe it's not true.*" The "*if*" in verse 6 is a first class condition, which indicates that the statement it controls is true. (". . *if we hold fast the confidence and rejoicing of hope firm to the end*" – which we will!") Notice that the statement does not say "*Whose house we shall be.*" It says, "*whose house we are*" right now.

We could illustrate the meaning this way: suppose somebody came to you with a plant bulb in his hand and said, "*Is this a tulip bulb?*" Suppose you did not know, but you replied, "*I'm not sure, but if you plant it in the ground and it produces a tulip blossom next spring, then it is, right now, a tulip bulb.*" It would not become a tulip bulb while growing. Its blossom would simply prove what it had always been. That is the sense of "if" in verse 6b.

Verses 7-9:

"*Therefore, as the Holy Spirit says: "Today, if you will hear His voice, 8 do not harden your hearts as in the rebellion, in the day of trial in the wilderness, 9 where your fathers tested Me, proved Me, and saw My works forty years."*"

Here is a quotation from Psalm 95:7-11. It points back to Numbers 13 and 14, where we find the dramatic account of Israel's great dereliction of faith. Brought by God, through a series of miracles, to the very verge of the promised land, their fear overcame their faith and they shrank from moving forward to take the prize. That was what the Psalmist called "*The provocation*", or "*the rebellion.*" God was provoked to anger by the failure of His people to trust Him for what He had promised. Consequently, with the exception of Joshua and Caleb, the entire generation perished in the wilderness.

That is the principle behind the teaching of Hebrews 3 and 4. It is a story of tragedy, in which a whole generation of God's people, who had seen God work in mighty ways, and had even heard the sound of His voice, lost the prize because they refused to believe that "*what God had promised He was also able to perform.*" Here in verses 7-9 we find an appeal for us not to repeat their mistake. Unfortunately, multitudes of true believers settle for a wilderness experience instead of believing God for the "promised land." For us, of course, the Promised Land does not consist of real estate but of a relationship with Him who affords us rest and security. It is a relationship that is characterized by joy, love, trust and fruit. It is promised to us just as surely as the land was promised to Israel but we are expected to take it by faith. Nobody will achieve it in his own strength. That is where Israel failed. They calculated that they were not physically strong enough to defeat the inhabitants of Canaan and discounted the fact that God had promised to give them the land by His own power. That is how many Christians fail today. They see the kind of life that is described in the Scriptures and would very much like to live it, but instead of trusting God for it they try to attain it by their own efforts. In doing so, they are bound to fail. Paul wrote to the Colossians: *"As you have received Christ Jesus the Lord, so walk in Him."* How did we receive Him? By faith alone. How, then, are we to walk in Him? The same way -- by faith alone!

"If"

The *"if"* in verse 7 is not a first class condition (as it was in verse 6) but a third class condition, which means *"maybe you will hear His voice and maybe you will not."* Some will and some will not. Another interesting fact is that in the Hebrew Psalm, the *"He"* points back to Jehovah, while in the New Testament Greek it refers to the Lord Jesus. This makes Jehovah of the Old Testament the same as Jesus in the New. At the beginning of the book we read that God has spoken to us through His Son and that therefore we should give earnest heed to what He has said. In other words, we are to *"hear His voice."* However, this will not happen automatically. There is a condition for hearing Him. It is simply that we must not harden our hearts as Israel did in the wilderness. At Kadesh-Barnea, Israel "heard" the Lord's voice through Moses, Joshua and Caleb, all of whom bore witness to the fact that God had promised to give them the land regardless of their own weakness. But Israel was blinded by the vision of walled cities and warlike tribes, and refused to trust God to carry out His promise. God said, *"Go! I have prepared the way for you."* But they said, *"No! We don't have the strength or the means."*

In the medical profession there are two Greek words in regular use. One is "schlerosis" (which refers to the hardening of tissue) and the other is "cardiac" (which pin-points symptoms relating to the heart). Both words are used in verse 8. "Arterial schlerosis" is the hardening of the arteries, which hinders the flow of life-giving blood to the body. Here we have "cardiac schlerosis," the hardening of the heart, which hinders the power of God's Word from reaching the soul. Both result in weakness, one physical and the other spiritual.

Verses 10-11:

"Therefore I was angry with that generation, and said, 'They always go astray in their heart, and they have not known My ways.' 11 So I swore in My wrath, 'They shall not enter My rest.'"

Notice that God did not speak of "*Your* rest", but of "*My* rest." It is a place belonging specifically to God. It is where God is and always has been. His rest is the product of His total control over all things. There is no apprehension there because He is never taken by surprise. There is no fear there because He is never threatened. There is no guilt there because He has never sinned and there is no regret there because He is never wrong. In other words, His rest is a place based solely on the attributes of His own character. It is God's desire that we rest in Him and live in total dependence upon Him. Most of us are mesmerized by the scope of our assignment and the strength of the odds ranged against us. They seem overwhelming and we feel impotent. We just don't have the strength or the will-power to overcome our own blemishes, let alone cope with the enemy. But by thinking that way, we simply repeat the mistakes of Israel when they stood on the verge of the Promised Land and shut ourselves out of the blessing being offered to them.

The danger of a hardened heart

Verse 12:

"Beware, brethren, lest there be in any of you an evil heart of unbelief in departing from the living God."

The unbelief referred to here is simply unwillingness to trust God. The promise of rest has been made. It is offered, free of charge and with no conditions. But God will not negotiate. His position is absolute. He waits for us to embrace His offer and if we refuse, we "depart" from Him. He will not run after us. By that I mean that He will not change His terms to accommodate us. We either accept His offer or repeat the "provocation" of ancient Israel. If we refuse His "rest", we will experience conflict, just as Israel experienced conflict in "the waste and howling wilderness," when they could have been enjoying the "land flowing with milk and honey." God will not condemn us, or punish us for refusing His gift, but we will hurt ourselves. As an illustration, if we were to jump from a tall building, we would be injured when we struck the ground. This would not be God's judgment upon us. It would be the logical and inevitable result of our own action. Likewise, if we refuse to trust God's offer of spiritual rest, the logical result will be conflict.

Two qualities must be present within us before we can enjoy God's blessing -- obedience and faith. One without the other is neutralized. Faith without obedience is presumption; obedience without faith is bondage. Cain demonstrated faith without obedience when he approached God on his own terms instead of the terms which God had clearly laid down. He then became angry with his brother when God rejected him. He was presumptuous. Many people today have the same attitude. They want to be friends with God; they want to know Him, but they set up their own terms and believe, in their pride, that God will somehow make an exception in their case. But He will not. His terms are the same for everyone, and although He is perfect love, He will not change them to suit our personal viewpoint. The modern philosophy of life, in which everyone has a right to be heard and everyone's viewpoint must be considered, does not apply to God. He says, *"This is my way, walk in it and I will give you rest."* All the faith in the world is of no value without obedience.

On the other hand, obedience without faith results in the worst kind of bondage. Nobody is more miserable than the person who tries to live the Christians life without resting in the Lord. It results in a grim, powerless, joyless legalism. The Christian life was never designed to be lived on the basis of clenched teeth and iron will. Any attempt to do so will result in spiritual disillusionment and exhaustion. There must be a balanced combination of faith and obedience if we wish to avoid this deadly "hardening of our hearts."

Verse 13:

"but exhort one another daily, while it is called "Today", lest any of you be hardened through the deceitfulness of sin."

My wife and I once took a group of teenagers on a week's hike around Mount Hood in the Oregon Cascades. The going was steep and we were carrying seven days-worth of supplies on our backs, which weighed us down. Some fell behind. A couple of them even said they could go no further and we should leave them there to die! But the others stayed with them, relieved them of their packs and coaxed them on until they reached the goal. The result was a feeling of exhilaration for all. That is the spirit which should pervade the Christian body.

We are all charged with the responsibility of encouraging our neighbors, lest sin gain the advantage. The definition of sin is *"missing the mark"* and if we fail to claim God's rest, we miss the mark which He sets for us. Thus, we sin. Sin is deceitful because we are frequently unaware that we are refusing God's offer. We think we are doing fine and are therefore tricked into missing God's best. We need to remind and be reminded of the blessing which is available to us. The present window of opportunity is referred to as *"Today"* and points back to Psalm 95:7, which we noted earlier.

Partakers with Christ

Verse 14:

"For we have become partakers of Christ if we hold the beginning of our confidence steadfast to the end."

Once again we find a first class condition for the word *"if"*. It means, *"If, and the statement is true."* In other words, we are made partakers of Christ (right now). We don't have to wait until the end to find out if we have passed the exam. When I went to school, the English system did work that way. Yearly grades were not counted. Everything depended on one final exam, which obviously created considerable stress. But God's system is not like that. Romans 8:16-17 makes it clear that we are made partakers of Christ the moment we believe. The statement in this verse provides proof, not condition. It describes the evidence that a person really is a partaker of Christ. Holding our confidence steadfast to the end will be living proof that we entered into an eternal relationship when we received Christ.

Verses 15-18:

". . while it is said: "Today, if you will hear His voice, do not harden your hearts as in the rebellion." 16 For who, having heard, rebelled? Indeed, was it not all who came out of Egypt, led by Moses? 17 Now with whom was He angry forty years? Was it not with those who sinned, whose corpses fell in the wilderness? 18 And to whom did He swear that they would not enter His rest, but to those who did not obey? 19 So we see that they could not enter in because of unbelief."

Here the writer takes us back again to the story of Israel's failure at Kadesh Barnea. It is a dramatic illustration of the fallacy that the majority is always right. Most of the time it is wrong! At Kadesh, God turned back a whole nation and rewarded two men. The majority could have received what Joshua and Caleb received, had they disregarded the logical evidence and trusted God instead, but they hardened their hearts and consequently missed the opportunity. It all boiled down to unbelief. However, we must keep in mind that the nation was made up of individuals. Each person had the opportunity to stand with Joshua and Caleb. They were individuals too. There could have been six, or twenty or a thousand others of their generation standing with the two, but there were not. Out of the entire population of people from the age of twenty years old and up, only those two stood firm against the odds and reaped the reward. Don't ever imagine that a thing is right because "everyone is doing it", or "everyone believes it." Most likely, if "everyone" is doing or believing something it will be wrong.

It is frequently difficult to apply what seems to be abstract truth to everyday living. The two seem to occupy different realms. By abstract truth I mean truth which cannot be touched or proved with the senses. This whole passage is dealing with the subject of entering into God's "rest", which may seem to be abstract. Here I am, living in a real world, surrounded by real people, doing a real job and supporting a real family. How do I put the practical and the abstract together? Well, to begin with, there was nothing abstract about Israel's situation at Kadesh Barnea. The people were faced with a practical decision. The folks over the border were fierce. They lived in walled cities and possessed modern weaponry. They would fervently defend their country and the Israelites knew that they were no match for them. On the other hand, God was saying *"Take your women and children and go in anyway. Discount the strength of the opposition. I will give you the land."* It was a gut-wrenching decision to make. What would they do? Would they lean to their own understanding or trust God? Trusting God involved being vulnerable. It involved risking their lives and future on a project for which they had no guarantee of survival (let alone victory) other than the "abstract" promise of God. We know what they decided and we know what happened as the result.

We are sometimes faced with similar decisions in our own lives. Will I trust my own ability to order my life or will I trust the Lord to lead me His way? By deciding to trust God, I may find myself vulnerable. The world will not understand. It will think me strange. It will say that I am sacrificing common sense for "religion." But so what? Are they right or is God right? I know who I would rather trust!

There is another truth that comes out of the Kadesh Barnea story. Although Joshua and Caleb were faithful and did not harden their hearts like the rest of the people, they still had to wait forty years before claiming their inheritance. We tend to desire instant results, don't we? (*"I prayed, I believed, I obeyed, so why has God not opened the door?"*) God's timing is not always the same as ours. I am sure Joshua and Caleb were disappointed at being turned back, but I am also sure they learned valuable lessons while they awaited the fulfillment of the promise. We never lose out when we trust God. It may seem that we do but God knows His business and He never wastes experiences. He uses them to good advantage later on.

During my early years I experienced many things, which I felt did not help me in my desire for ministry. I had farm experience, college experience, hard work in a mine and in the woods, and I wondered how these things could prepare me for the call I believed God had given me. But when God placed my wife and I in the villages we soon discovered that every one of those experiences was valuable. I could milk the cows for farmers who were sick or injured, I could understand the viewpoint of the laborer because I had walked in his shoes, and I could identify with the academic world because I had been there also. God does not waste experiences. Should you feel that you have been sidelined for a

CHAPTER 4

This chapter continues to stress the concept of spiritual rest, which dominated chapter 3. As we have seen, the writer uses the word *"rest"* to describe total trust and dependence on the Lord. We "rest" in a chair or on a bed. We do not question its ability to support us. We simply commit our body to its keeping and relax. That is the physical equivalent of the spiritual commitment spotlighted in these chapters. If I rest in the Lord, I reject the idea that the success of my daily walk "all depends on me" and cease from my own struggles. I reject the notion that I am supposed to "live my life for Christ", and instead I consciously allow Him to live His life in me. I take Christ's statement, *"Without me you can do nothing,"* seriously, and believe that Paul's statement, *"I was crucified with Christ; nevertheless I live, yet not I, but Christ lives in me,"* is literally true. In other words, I rest in Him and He now lives His life through me.

Spiritual rest

Verse 1:

"Therefore, since a promise remains of entering His rest, let us fear lest any of you seem to have come short of it."

Just as the promise of physical rest was made to every individual in Israel at Kadesh Barnea, so the promise of spiritual rest is made to every believer. This intimate relationship with Christ is not a prize, intended only for a few super-saints to achieve. It is what God wants every Christian to enjoy. The promise is given to the lowliest of saints, and if we fail to grasp it, we simply deny ourselves the blessing that is intended for us. It is ours for the asking and God desires us to enjoy it.

Paul's statement in 1 Thessalonians 5:18, *"In everything give thanks, for this is the will of God in Christ Jesus concerning you,"* bears witness to this state of rest. If we are truly trusting God to undertake in every facet of our lives, we can be sure that everything that happens to us along the way (even things which we consider to be negative) has been allowed by Him, for our own benefit. With that knowledge, we can thank Him in all circumstances, because His perfect will is being carried out, whether we understand it or not.

Verse 2:

"For indeed the gospel was preached to us as well as to them; but the word which they heard did not profit them, not being mixed with faith in those who heard it."

We all know that the word *"gospel"* means *"good news."* So what good news was preached to the Israelites in Moses' day? It was not the good news of salvation because that was a mystery not yet revealed. No, the good news preached to the Israelites concerned the "rest" that God intended them to enjoy in Canaan. God said, *"Here is your inheritance; go in and claim it."* However, *"the word preached did not profit them, not being mixed with faith in those who heard it."* The Gospel, to them, was wasted, not because the promise was false, or unattainable, but because the people did not believe it.

We are not considering "heaven-when-we-die" here. All who have trusted Jesus Christ as their Savior already have that. This gospel refers to the close relationship with Christ, which is offered to all believers in this life. It is offered to all who will claim it, but like salvation itself, it can be grasped only by faith. It is invisible, inaudible and intangible. We may experience it only by believing the promise and standing upon it.

Verse 3a:

"For we who have believed do enter that rest . . ."

"We", there, includes the writer. He had believed and had entered into the experience he was describing. His desire was that his readers might enjoy the blessing he had discovered. Saving faith gets us out of Egypt, so to speak, but it does not get us into the Promised Land. Salvation has to do with heaven-when-we-die, while "rest" has to do with this life

as we walk it, day by day. It is not a "second blessing." It is already ours when we become Christians, but we experience it only when we change our thinking about life in general. The crises, dangers, sicknesses and sadness will still be there. They will not go away. People will still be difficult, children will still play up and things will still go wrong. But if we are to find the "rest" described in this passage, we must come to a genuine understanding that there is nothing we can do to control our circumstances. Fretting and worrying over them will not help. We must take our eyes off our circumstances and switch our focus to the One who *is* able to control all things. We must yield to Him and say, "*Lord, you take over. I am going to rest in you. I am going to quit struggling and allow you to work things out the way you know best. Here are the keys, now you drive!*" In this regard, Psalm 37 is a wonderful passage to commit to memory.

Verse 3b:

". . as He has said: "So I swore in My wrath, they shall not enter My rest," although the works were finished from the foundation of the world."

What work was finished before the foundation of the world? He referred to the work of creation, the calling into existence of all physical and finite things. There was a point in eternity when time began. We do not know when the clock began to run, but we might assume that it commenced at the time of creation, when the solar system was flung into space and all things that we now hear, see, touch, taste and smell were brought into being by the Word of God. However, the creation included more than finite things. When God created man, for instance, He also brought into being an eternal soul, containing a whole new universe of emotions, needs and yearnings, which only God could satisfy. He knew then that man would sin, and by sinning, wreck the balance which kept the sensitive soul at peace with his Maker. Thus, the plan of salvation and the way of rest were already designed and perfected before the physical creation took place. The Lamb was slain before the foundation of the world, the saints were chosen before the foundation of the world, and here we read that the "*works*" were completed before the foundation of the world. It is obvious from the context of this passage that God's "rest" is in view. The connection is explained in the next verses.

Verse 4:

"For He has spoken in a certain place of the seventh day in this way: "And God rested on the seventh day from all His works."

Why did God rest on the seventh day? Was He tired? Did He say to Himself, *"I'm so weary after all my work that I must take a break and catch up on my rest?"* A notion like that would be inconsistent with the revealed character of God in Scripture. God is omnipotent, eternal and perfect. He is the source of all energy and power. Weariness is a human problem, not a divine one. So why did God rest on the seventh day? Simply because there was nothing else to do! The work was finished; the universe was complete. Man was created, salvation was prepared and the way of rest was finalized. There remained only one factor to be dealt with, and that was man's volition. Man had to enter into the finished work of God on the basis of faith before he could enjoy it.

The remainder of this passage explains three things: 1. The people under Moses failed to enter into any kind of rest; 2. The people under Joshua, 40 years later, entered into only a physical, temporal rest; 3. David, writing 500 years after the occupation of Canaan, was still offering rest to the people of God, saying *"Today you can enter in, provided you don't repeat the sin of Israel, which was unbelief."* Much of this is repetition, but when Scriptures repeat themselves it is evidence that the material is important.

Verses 5-9:

". . . and again in this place: "They shall not enter My rest." 6 Since therefore it remains that some must enter it, and those to whom it was first preached did not enter because of disobedience, 7 again He designates a certain day, saying in David, "Today," after such a long time, as it has been said: "Today, if you will hear His voice, do not harden your hearts." 8 For if Joshua had given them rest, then He would not afterward have spoken of another day. 9 There remains therefore a rest for the people of God."

Admittedly, that passage is rather labored, but the truth it proclaims is clear enough. God did not allow Moses' generation to enter His "rest" because of their unbelief. Nevertheless, He obviously intended His people to enjoy the blessing, or David would not have been offering it to his readers 500 years later. The statement at the end of verse 7 is a new angle. If Joshua's generation had enjoyed the complete fulfillment of God's promise after occupying Canaan, the blessing would not still be offered today. But it is offered, and is obviously still current. (To avoid possible confusion, if you are using the King James Bible you will see "*Jesus*" in verse 8 instead of "*Joshua*." "*Joshua*" is the correct interpretation. Joshua is the Old Testament rendering of Jesus).

Verse 10:

"For he who has entered His rest has himself also ceased from his works as God did from His."

There is the key. You can't work and rest at the same time, can you? You have to choose one or the other. Resting involves turning responsibility over into God's hands and allowing Him to work things out His way. The Bible admonishes us to "*be anxious for nothing.*" That is a tall order if we are running our own affairs. We shall certainly be anxious if we imagine that everything depends upon us. The only way to avoid anxiety is to surrender responsibility for the outcome to God. Joshua hit a giant-sized problem at Jericho. Huge walls surrounded the city and armed men manned them. Joshua probably envisioned a sickening number of casualties when he attacked. However, just before the battle, Joshua met Christ and found himself lying on his face before Him. He yielded command to the "Captain of the Lord's host" and the walls fell without a blow being struck. It was a mighty victory, but it was not Joshua's victory. Nor was it Israel's victory. It was God's victory and that is how it should always be.

Verse 11:

"Let us therefore be diligent to enter that rest, lest anyone fall after the same example of disobedience."

The writer closes out this section with an appeal to his readers. Having trusted Christ for salvation, why miss out on this place of blessing which is offered to all believers. Why struggle with the task of trying to please God when this place of rest is available to all who will reach out and claim it?

Chapter 4

The Word of God

Verse 12:

"For the word of God is living and powerful, and sharper than any two-edged sword, piercing even to the division of soul and spirit, and of joints and marrow, and is a discerner of the thoughts and intents of the heart."

Here is a verse which is packed with information. In Hebrews 1:2 we were told that God has spoken (to us) through His Son. That communication is what we recognize as "the Word God." Here that Word is analyzed in detail. We are told what the Word *is* and what it *does*. Each of these two sections is split into several parts.

First, What God's word IS:

A. It is *alive.*

In what way is it alive? The Bible we hold in our hands is not alive. It consists only of words printed on paper. However, the truth it communicates goes much deeper than paper and ink. As an illustration, when we say that a living thing has died, we mean that the spirit of life has departed from it. This spirit is indefinable. No-one has ever seen pure life. We observe what it does and how it behaves. We see how it affects the organisms in which it resides, but life itself remains a mystery. It is the invisible activating force within the organism, and the basic difference between a living thing and a dead thing is that one functions while the other does not. There is also a difference between physical life and spiritual life. One functions in the sphere of physics while the other functions in the sphere of the spirit. The two are independent of one another. Someone who is physically alive may be spiritually dead, and someone who is physically dead can be spiritually alive.

The Word of God, as we hold it in our hands, is technically dead. It has no physical life. It does not breathe, it does not eat, it does not drink and it does not move. It does not function independently in the world of physics. However, Jesus said, in John 6:63, *"The words that I speak to you, they are spirit and they are life."* So what are *"words?"* Spoken words are merely a system of sounds, designed to convey thought.

Written words are the grouping of characters, designed to do the same thing. Had we actually heard Jesus speak, most of us would have been unable to understand Him because He spoke in Aramaic. Yet His words would still have been "spirit," and they would have still been "life." Our ability, or inability, to understand them would not have changed their character.

The "life" of God's Word does not reside in its sound or in its appearance, but in the truth which it conveys. The Word of God is alive spiritually in that what it says is energized by the Holy Spirit and applied, on a spiritual level, to the hearts of men and women. There is a convicting power in the Word of God, which lies in no other document, because the *Word* of God is the *will* of God. In Matthew 12:34, the Lord Jesus said, "*Out of the abundance of the heart the mouth speaks.*" What does the mouth speak? Words! Our words reveal our hearts, and the Bible is the Word of God. He caused it to be written and He decided how its truth should be phrased. "*Holy men of God spoke as they were moved by the Holy Ghost.*" Therefore, the Scriptures reveal the heart of God

 B. It is *powerful.*

We read in Genesis 1:3 that "*God said, Let there be light, and there was light.*" Then, in verses 6, 9, 11, 14, 20, 24 and 26, He spoke the word again and His will was done. No angel could have demonstrated such power. Isaiah 40:8 reads,"*The grass withers, the flower fades, but the Word of our God stands forever.*" When Jesus stood at the tomb of the dead Lazarus, He just said, "*Lazarus, come forth,*" and at His command Lazarus rose from the dead. Peter wrote in 2 Peter 3:5-7, "*For this they willingly forget: that by the word of God the heavens were of old, and the earth standing out of the water and in the water, 6 by which, the world that then existed perished, being flooded with water. 7 But the heavens and the earth which are now preserved by the same word, are reserved for fire until the day of judgment and perdition of ungodly men.*" The Lord has controlled all things with His word from the beginning of time and will continue to control it with His word until time comes to an end. The word of God is the most powerful force ever to exist, infinitely beyond the earthquake, the tsunami, the hurricane or the whirlwind. On the Sea of Galilee, the Lord merely said "*Peace, be still*" and the storm ceased its raging, like a dog coming to heel.

C. It is *sharp*.

God's Word is sharper than any two-edged sword. The word *"sword"* in this instance is *"machaira"*, which was the short-sword used by the Roman legionaries. Someone has said that this was the secret weapon of the day. Much of the success enjoyed by the Roman armies, as they conquered nation after nation, was attributable to this deadly weapon. It was short, light, with two edges and a sharp point. It could cut right and left, and pierce without causing the soldier to lose balance, enabling him to run circles round the enemy, who was usually equipped with the more conventional single-bladed weapon. God's Word is like that. In Ephesians 6:17 it is called *"the sword of the Spirit"*-- the weapon which the Spirit uses!

The first word of verse 12 is *"For"*, meaning *"Because"*. This ties it in with the previous paragraph, which has to do with entering (or failing to enter) God's rest. As a reminder, verse 11 reads, *"Let us labor therefore to enter into that rest, lest any man fall after the same example of unbelief."* Then, verse 12 begins, *"For (because) the word of God is alive and powerful, and sharper than any two-edged sword."* The connection is that God's Word is more than sufficient to give us victory over the things that would keep us out of God's rest. When Satan attacked Jesus in the wilderness (Matthew 4) Jesus used the word as His weapon and Satan was defeated. Paul wrote in 2 Corinthians 10:3-5: *"For though we walk after the flesh, we do not war after the flesh, 4 for the weapons of our warfare are not carnal, but mighty through God to the pulling down of strongholds, 5 casting down arguments and every high thing that exalts itself against the knowledge of God, bringing every thought into captivity to the obedience of Christ."*

That brings us to the second section of verse 12. We have seen what the word *is* (alive, powerful and sharp). Now we shall see:

What God's Word DOES:

A. It *divides*.

It divides between soul and spirit. What does that mean? How can God's Word make a division like that? To grasp that we must first understand the terms used. The spirit is the highest part of man, the seat of *God*-consciousness. It is on the wavelength of the spirit that we communicate with him and he with us. Romans 8:16 says that *"the Spirit bears witness with our spirit that we are children of God."* The soul, on the other hand, is the ego, the seat of *self*-consciousness. This part of man is very strong and often comes to the fore, pushing the spirit into the background. The body, of course, is simply the temporary house in which both soul and spirit reside. The bodies of believers will be changed and raised when the Lord returns.

When Adam was created, God gave him a body, a soul and a spirit. In his body, he was able to function in this world. With his soul, he was able to appreciate beauty and enjoy the delights of Eden. With his spirit, he was able to commune with God. When he sinned, he died spiritually. His spirit no longer functioned as it was created to do. He fell to the level of the soul. In effect, man changed from a trichotomous being to a dichotomous being and lost contact with God. It was as if a telephone line had been cut. In 1 Corinthians 2:14, the unregenerate man is called (literally) "the *soulish* man," because he is dominated by his emotions. In fact, the word *"psychology"* comes from the Greek word for soul. This is a correct label because psychology is limited to the soul of man (which is degenerate) and it is unable to touch the spirit. That is why psychology is largely ineffective. It tries to fix up the old nature and make it better. Even God does not attempt to do that. Paul said, *"In me, that is, in my flesh, there dwells no good thing,"* and he was right.

The only hope for lost man is for him to be pronounced dead and replaced with a new man. Only God can do that. Like fallen Adam, the unsaved man has a spirit but it is inactive. When a person is saved, God literally "divides the soul from the spirit" and raises it to its proper place, where it can function as it was originally intended to do. God activates the telephone line, and He does that by means of the Word. *"Faith comes by hearing and hearing by the word of God."* As Arthur Pink puts it, *"The spirit is raised from its immersion in the soul, and once more functions separately."* The Word of God (energized by the Holy Spirit) penetrates the soul of the person who is being regenerated and divides (rescues, if you like) the spirit from the domination of the soul. Only then can a person rest in Christ, because rest is the exercise of faith, and faith is a gift from God.

Unfortunately, that is seldom the end of things because a battle immediately ensues between the spirit (prompted by God) and the soul (which is still under the control of the emotions and will). As Galatians 5:17 puts it: "*The flesh lusts against the spirit, and the spirit against the flesh; and these are contrary the one to the other.*" Someone might challenge that and claim that the soul is different from the flesh because the soul can be saved while the flesh cannot be. That is true, but it is also true that the lusts of the flesh are resident in the soul, not in the spirit. The spirit of a Christian never rebels against the will of God. Rebellion comes from within the soul. It is the will and the emotions that are "*soulish*", not the spirit, and it is there that the Christian finds himself in trouble. If the soul is allowed to take the upper hand, the Christian's spirituality begins to deteriorate because his emotions, likes and dislikes begin to dictate his behavior. The believer is still a believer. He has not lost his salvation. He still attends church and does all the things Christians are supposed to do, but his profession becomes empty. Without correction, his thought patterns and attitudes will become similar to those of someone who has never trusted Christ.

The remedy, in almost every case, is the Word of God. Usually, it has been neglected. The *reading* of it may not have been neglected. Many "soulish" Christians routinely read a portion of Scripture every day, but it does them little good because they do not allow it to speak to their hearts. Only as we meditate on God's Word and allow the Spirit of God to speak to us through it will it divide between soul and spirit and banish the emotions and will to the place where they belong. Obviously, there is a place for emotions and will, but they must be surrendered to (and controlled by) God in order to function as they were created to function.

This verse also says that the Word divides between the joints and the marrow. Like the soul and the spirit, the joints and the marrow are both inward things. You can't see them. The joints lie within the flesh and the marrow lies within the bone. Here they are used figuratively, of course. Obviously the joints and the marrow are not physically affected by the word of God, but the writer is stressing its penetrating nature.

Finally, we are told that the Word *discerns*.

It is "*a discerner of the thoughts and intents of the heart.*" The word translated "*discerner*" is "*kritikos*" or critic. It signifies one who is skilled at judging. In this case, it is the inner thought-pattern that is under scrutiny. The Word convicts of sin and causes the sinner to repent. Actually, this last idea is best developed in the next verse"

God's omniscience

Verse 13:

"*And there is no creature hidden from His sight, but all things are naked and open to the eyes of Him to whom we must give account.*"

Our thoughts, our attitudes, our likes, our dislikes, our joys, our fears, our secret longings, are all open to the gaze of God. We have no secrets from Him. He knows us absolutely as we are – all the good things and all the bad things -- just as if they were all spread out on a table under a bright light. The wonderful thing is that He loves us, just the same! Some people think they can hide from God, like Adam did after he sinned, but it is useless to try. Others imagine that by acting in a pious manner they can hoodwink God into believing that all is well. But God is never hoodwinked. Psalm 139 is a wonderful commentary on this. David wrote:

"*O Lord, you have searched me and known me. You know my downsitting and my uprising, you understand my thought afar off. You surround my path and my lying down and are acquainted with all my ways. For there is not a word on my tongue, but Lord, you know it altogether.*"

Then he asked:

"*Where shall I go from your Spirit? Where shall I flee from your presence? If I ascend up into Heaven, you are there. If I make my bed in sheol, you are there. If I take the wings of the morning and dwell in the uttermost parts of the sea, even there shall your hand lead me. . . .*"

"*If I say, Surely the darkness shall hide me, even the night shall*

> *be light about me. . .The darkness and the light are both alike to you."*

God is omniscient, He knows everything, and His Word demonstrates it. People like to think that they are sophisticated and advanced in knowledge today. They call the Bible "simplistic," and claim that modern society has progressed beyond the scope of its teaching. Yet *"professing themselves to wise, they become fools."* Although the Scriptures were written in a bygone age, when its characters knew nothing of cars, or planes, or computers, or atom bombs, they describe the nature of man with pin-point accuracy, and diagnose his problems more clearly than any modern medical or psychological text book. God *knows* us, better than we know ourselves.

The last phrase of verse 13 is particularly sobering. *". . to whom we must give account."* (KJV: *"with whom we have to do."*) Literally, the phrase says, *"with whom is our word"* (logos). Verse 12 is all about the Word of God, and verse 13 closes with a reference to our word. The idea of "giving account" comes from the fact that a steward is answerable vocally to his master. (See the parable of the Talents, Matthew 25:14-30). There will come a day when every one of us will stand before our Maker and answer verbally for our stewardship. Our salvation will not be in peril but our rewards will be (1 Corinthians 3:11-15).

To some, the thought of this inevitable encounter with Christ is terrifying. Not only have they grown up with the idea that God is stern and judgmental, but they are conscious (as we all are) of wrong within. They feel that they are quite unprepared to meet their Creator, and are consequently convicted that such a confrontation would be disastrous. To any who find themselves in this group, the final three verses of chapter 4 should provide relief because they explain the basis upon which we may have boldness in the presence of the Lord, and the ground upon which we may claim His mercy and grace.

The great High Priest

Verse 14:

"Seeing then that we have a great High Priest who has passed through the heavens, Jesus the Son of God, let us hold fast our confession."

Jesus, the Son of God, is presented here, not as our judge, but as our high priest. The High Priest of Bible times occupied a very important position. Moses' brother, Aaron, was the first High Priest, and God was specific about his responsibilities. Two precious stones were engraved with the names of the twelve tribes of Israel, six on each, and placed upon his shoulders. He was appointed to carry them before the Lord as a memorial. The names of the twelve tribes were also engraved on twelve other stones and fastened to his breastplate. He was to carry them upon his heart. Symbolically, he represented all the people before God. It was Aaron's responsibility to go alone into the Holy of Holies – into the very presence of God – and make atonement for the people. He was their personal representative. When the writer to the Hebrews speaks here of "our great High Priest" he is referring to One appointed by God, who personally and exclusively represents our interests before the great throne of the universe in Heaven.

This verse also refers to the heavens. "Our great High Priest has passed *"through the heavens."* It is important that we understand the significance of this phrase. There are two areas which are assigned similar names, but which are quite distinct from one another. One is *"Heaven"* and the other is *"the heavens."* *"Heaven"* is the abode of God, whereas *"the heavens"* refers to the stellar universe, part of which we see in the night sky.

In Old Testament times, the High Priest (and only the High Priest) once per year, on the Day of Atonement, took the blood of the sacrifice from the altar through the court of the tabernacle, through the Holy Place, past the veil, and into the Holy of Holies. There He sprinkled the blood on the Mercy Seat as atonement (or settlement) for the sins of the people. Nobody but the High Priest dare pass the veil. Had they done so they would have died instantly. But not until the blood had been sprinkled was the transaction complete. That was the shadow of the real thing. It was a picture of the Lord Jesus who would one day come to this earth and offer Himself as the final atonement. In the fullness of time, the shadow became reality. Christ died at Calvary; His own blood was poured out as a settlement for sin, once for all. But the transaction was not technically complete until He presented Himself at the Mercy Seat in glory, which is the throne of God. Hebrews 9:12 reads: *"Neither by the blood of goats and calves, but by His own blood He entered in once into the Holy Place, having obtained eternal redemption for us."*

In order to do this, Jesus passed *through the heavens.* This was Satan's territory. He is *"The prince of the power of the air,"* and the word *"air"* specifically refers to the atmospheric envelope surrounding this earth. Thus, the victorious Christ passed through Satan's kingdom. The power of Satan opposed Him as He went, but could not prevent Him. Colossians 2:15 says, *"And having spoiled the principalities and the powers* (both *"principalities"* and *"powers"* have the definite article, indicating the specific forces of Satan described in Ephesians 6:12) *He made an open shame of them, triumphing over them."* The word *"spoiled"* there means *"to wholly strip off from one's self, to disarm."* It describes the unseen battle in the skies when Satan and his forces attempted to hinder Christ as He passed through their territory on His way to the Mercy Seat of God. He *"stripped off"* from Himself their efforts to impede His progress and openly demonstrated their inability to do so. Since this was accomplished, and Christ is now at the right hand of God . . . *"let us hold fast our confession!"*

We "have" Him (verse 14) because He is there, representing us before God, pleading our cause, even when we waver, even when we are "soulish" and fail, even when we are disgusted with ourselves and our failure, He is there and He is ours because He died for us and now ever lives to intercede on our behalf! It is a small thing to ask that we confess Him. *"Hold fast"* is in the continuing tense, which admonishes us to *"keep on confessing"* our faith in Him.

Someone might say, "But you don't know how weak I am. You don't know how difficult my life is. You don't know how prone I am to waver and fall. It is so hard to keep a good confession!" And that may be very true. But look at the next verse:

Verse 15:

"For we do not have a High Priest who cannot be touched (sympathize) with our weaknesses, but was in all points tempted as we are, yet without sin."

He understands; He remembers what it is like to walk in our shoes. He has lived in a human body and experienced the whole range of human feelings and emotions. He has laughed and wept. He has been tired, hungry, thirsty, forsaken, humiliated and angered. He has been betrayed and lied about, has experienced intense pain and even death. He has carved wood, cooked meals, washed feet, attended weddings and funerals. He has watched the sun rise and set, gone fishing, attended services, learned Scripture and tended to the needs of small brothers and sisters. He understands because He has been there. The only thing Christ did not experience in this life was sin, and that is the meaning of the last phrase of verse 15: *"Yet without sin."* The word, *"yet"* is not in the text. It was inserted by the translators. It just says, *"without sin."* However, we must remember that, sinless though He was, the accumulated sins of the whole human race were lowered upon Him as He hung upon the cross. He *did* experience sin, in that sense, because He was literally *"made to be sin"* when He took our place in judgment! The presence of such a High Priest, pleading our cause at the right hand of God, should give us confidence, no matter how often we stumble.

Verse 16:

"Let us therefore come boldly to the throne of grace, that we may obtain mercy and find grace to help in time of need."

That is where we belong – where mercy and grace abound. Mercy is the love that helps the wretched; grace is the love that pardons the guilty. We are all both wretched and guilty, and we need all the love and grace we can find. Need is ever with us, but our need is met in Christ. What hope do we have of entering into God's rest? Our hope is in the Lord -- in what He has done for us, in where He is and in why He is there. *"Times of need"* come upon us when we mistakenly think we are strong, but especially when doubts or crises or testing arise to try us, when we fail, or feel discouraged. It is at times like these when the knowledge of our High Priest's presence before the throne becomes most precious. Because He is there we may come boldly before the throne, confident that His intercession on our behalf is effective.

CHAPTER 5

Discussion regarding Israel's High Priest crosses the chapter break uninterrupted. Now, however, new material is added. In Exodus 28:30 we read,

> *"And you shall put in the breastplate of judgment the Urim and the Thummim, and they shall be over Aaron's heart when he goes in before the Lord. So Aaron shall bear the judgment of the children of Israel over his heart before the Lord continually."*

"Judgment", in that verse, does not mean judgment *upon* the people, but judgment (right decisions) *for* them. Today, nobody knows exactly what the Urim and Thummim were. Most scholars think they may have been stones of some sort. However, we do know that they were used to ascertain God's will for the people in specific instances. If a question of importance needed to be decided, the people approached the High Priest and he used the Urim and Thummim to determine the Lord's will in the matter. Because they were kept in a pocket within the High Priest's breastplate, the garment itself was called *"the breastplate of judgment."* God ordained that the High Priest was to carry them continually upon his heart. Obviously Aaron, and those who followed him, not only represented the people before God, but they also represented God before the people. In other words, the High Priest was the mediator, the go-between, between a sinful people and their holy God. And it was God, not the people, who appointed him to that office.

Verse 1:

> *"For every priest taken from among men is appointed for men in things pertaining to God, that he may offer both gifts and sacrifices for sins."*

The High Priest was taken from among men. He had to be one of them, fraught with their common weaknesses, in order to represent them. He was also ordained *"for men"*. That is, he was not his own. He was a public servant or minister. In addition his duty was to offer up gifts and sacrifices for sins. "Gifts and sacrifices" are the two basic expressions of devotion. Gifts speak of praise (which includes gratitude and thanksgiving), while sacrifices (the giving up of precious things) speak of repentance, (which includes confession and obedience). Both categories were given by the people and channeled through the High Priest, who offered them to God on their behalf.

Verses 2-3"

"He can have compassion on those who are ignorant and going astray, since he himself is also beset by weakness. 3 Because of this he is required as for the people, so also for himself, to offer for sins. "

Though ordained by God, the High Priest was still by nature a sinner. Therefore, as he set about his ministry he had to keep in mind that the sacrifices which he offered were as much for him as they were for the people he represented. Consequently, he was to be compassionate toward those whom he represented, without condoning their sin. If he ignored sin he would not be able to make atonement for it. On the other hand, he was not to be harsh or unreasonably severe. The principle was similar to that laid down in Galatians 6:1, which reads, *"Brethren, if any man be overtaken in a fault, you who are spiritual restore such a one in the spirit of meekness; considering yourself, lest you also are tempted."* Certainly, this did not describe Caiaphas or Annas, who were High Priests in Jesus' day, nor many others who held office through the years. They were not compassionate, but were mean-spirited and vindictive. This passage describes how God intended them to be. This was how God viewed the man who carried the welfare of his people on his heart and on his shoulders.

Appointed by God

Verse 4:

"And no man takes this honor to himself, but he who is called by God, just as Aaron was."

God did the choosing then, as He still does today. We don't decide our gifts or appoint ourselves to the ministry. That is why the Christian faith is termed a "calling," rather than an achievement. Jesus said, *"You did not choose me, but I chose you."* Therefore, the authority is His and the privilege is ours. Nobody deserves to be saved. We are saved by God's grace and called by His mercy.

After the order of Melchizedek

Verses 5-6:

"So also Christ did not glorify Himself to become High Priest, but it was He who said to Him: "You are My Son, today I have begotten You." 6 As He also says in another place: "You are a priest forever according to the order of Melchizedek".

The human priests were shadows of the great High Priest who was to come. His ministry fulfilled theirs and made them redundant. He was the fulfillment of the type, but even He did not appoint Himself. God appointed Him, first, as His Son, and second, as a priest forever. He completely outclassed the priesthood of Aaron and his descendents. Aaron died, while Jesus lives forever. Aaron's ministry was limited in scope, while the ministry of Jesus was complete. Aaron sacrificed animals as a shadow of what was to come; Jesus sacrificed Himself as the fulfillment of the type. Aaron was a sinner; Jesus was without sin. In fact, the Lord Jesus, while being the fulfillment of Aaron's type, belonged to a different order of priesthood altogether – the "order of Melchisedek." The significance of Melchisedek is dealt with fully in chapter 7. Suffice it to say here that he was a mysterious priest/king, who appeared to Abraham in Genesis 14 and received tithes from him. The lack of information on Melchisedek is used by the writer to the Hebrews to impress upon his readers the total supremacy of Christ's priesthood over all other types.

Verse 7:

"who, in the days of His flesh, when He had offered up prayers and supplications, with strong cries and tears to Him who was able to save Him from death, and was heard because of His godly fear."

We should remember that Christ was not just a passive actor in the drama of Calvary. He was a priest, performing the work which God had ordained Him to do. He offered up Himself as a deliberate act, just as intentional as the priest's action in killing the sacrificial animal. Jesus was not the unfortunate victim of a Jewish plot. That idea is nonsense. He came into the world to die. He was the fulfillment of the types, both of the priests and the sacrifice. He said, "*Therefore my Father loves me, because I lay down my life, that I might take it again. No man takes it from me, but I lay it down of myself. I have power to lay it down and I have power to take it again.*" (John 10:17-18). The Lord's death was a deliberate high priestly act, over which He exercised absolute control. His sacrifice was the supreme act of obedience to the Father's will.

So when did the occasion referred to in verse 7 take place? It almost has to be the events in the Garden of Gethsemane. The Gospels give us a very brief account of that dreadful time. They don't mention tears and they give us few details of the Lord's passion. However, the words "*prayers*", "*strong crying*" and "*tears*" speak of the intensity of the Lord's suffering on that occasion. We read that Jesus prayed, "*If it be possible, let this cup pass from me. Nevertheless, not as I will, but as you will.*" In one sense, that prayer was not granted. The "cup" to which Jesus referred did not pass from Him. He drank it to the dregs. But here in Hebrews 5:7 we read that Jesus prayed intensely to "*Him who was able to save Him from death, and **was heard** in that He feared.*" How could the writer claim that when we all know that Jesus was not saved from death? The answer lies in the literal meaning of the word translated "*from.*" The word (*ek*) means "*out of*" or "*out from.*" Jesus prayed to Him who was able to save Him *out from* death. He said, "*Father, into your hands I commend my spirit.*" Then He died, and for two days His body lay dead within the sealed tomb. But early on the third day the Father granted His prayer and Jesus rose from the dead.

The obedience of Christ

Verse 8:

> "*Though He was a Son, yet He learned obedience by the things which He suffered. 9 And having been perfected, He became the author of eternal salvation to all who obey Him.*"

Jesus "*learned* "obedience in the Garden of Gethsemane. If He was to fulfill the purpose for which He had come into this world, there was no way of avoiding the cross. He then *demonstrated* obedience at the cross. He could have called ten thousand angels to His side, but He did not do so. Having been perfected through obedience, He became the Author of eternal salvation – to a specific group of people. The group is comprised of "all who obey Him." He obeyed the Father; now it is for us to obey Him.

At this point, the subject matter of chapter 5 is interrupted and does not continue until the last verse of chapter 7. It is almost as though we come to a sign on the road marked "detour". Detours can be aggravating things, but there is usually a good reason for their being there. The road ahead is blocked in some way, which makes negotiating it difficult, if not impossible. It is therefore necessary to go round the obstruction and join the main road on the other side. That is what has happened here. In verse 6, we read that Christ is "*a priest forever after the order of Melkisedek*," and in verse 10 the statement is more or less repeated. That is where the road of reasoning is obstructed. The writer is obliged to make a detour due to the fact that he considers his readers unable to grasp his teaching.

Dull of hearing

Verses 10-11:

> (Jesus) "*called by God as High Priest according to the order of Melchizedek, 11 of whom* (that is of Melchisedek and Christ's fulfillment of his type) *we have much to say, and hard to explain, since you have become dull of hearing.*"

Arthur Pink writes that "to be dull of hearing is descriptive of the state of mind in which statements may be made without producing any corresponding impression." People with this problem hear spiritual truth but do not assimilate it. The information does not grip their minds because they are not really listening. Consequently, its impact is neutralized. Those who are "dull of hearing" often complain that the material is too heavy, or too deep. They prefer teaching or preaching that is lighter and more entertaining. This is usually not because they are new Christians. New Christians are ravenous for as much information as they can get. This is a condition into which believers may lapse due, as a rule, to the fact that they fail to use their spiritual muscles. Just as watching too much television dulls the intellect (because it demands no effort on the part of the watcher) so continual passive reception of spiritual truth dulls the spirit. It is difficult to teach people who have lapsed into that condition. Apparently, this is the state into which the Hebrew Christians had fallen. They had not always been like it. They had once been alert and receptive, but they had become dull of hearing through neglect.

The writer to the Hebrews had now come to what might be termed a "heavy part" of his argument. He wanted to compare Christ with the mysterious Melchisedek, but he felt that his readers were not spiritually ready to assimilate what he said. The next verses explain the problem more fully.

Verse 12-14:

"For though by this time you ought to be teachers, you need someone to teach you again the first principles of the oracles of God; and you have come to need milk and not solid food. 13 For everyone who partakes only of milk is unskilled in the word of righteousness, for he is a babe. 14 But solid food belongs to those who are of full age, that is, those who by reason of use have their senses exercised to discern both good and evil."

Obviously the original readers of this letter were not new Christians. They had been taught God's Word and should have progressed in their perception of spiritual truth. Instead, they had evidently stagnated and lost their spiritual edge. In fact, they needed to go back to the roots of their faith and begin growing all over again. During my years in the ministry I have known a great many people like that. They have been Christians for years but have no hunger for God's Word and no excitement about learning new truth. They have lapsed into a kind of doldrums in which routine is the most impelling facet of their experience. Sadly, this is a pit into which any of us could fall. All we need do is sit and soak, making no effort to move on and up in our relationship with the Savior.

CHAPTER 6

We come now to that dreaded passage in the letter to the Hebrews, which has filled countless generations of readers with unnecessary apprehension. Those of an Arminian persuasion have pointed triumphantly to it as "proof" that we can lose our salvation if we fail to maintain the correct standard of faith, though nobody has clarified exactly where the line is that must be crossed in order to bring judgment down upon us. On the other hand, those who hold to the Calvanistic teaching know for sure that it cannot mean what it seems to say because that would conflict with many other passages which clearly guarantee the security of the believer. So how do we read the passage?

On to maturity

Verses 1-2:

"Therefore, leaving the discussion of the elementary principles of Christ, let us go on to maturity, not laying again the foundation of repentance from dead works and of faith toward God, 2 of the doctrine of baptisms, of laying on of hands, of resurrection of the dead, and of eternal judgment."

The key to this passage is at the beginning of verse 1. *"Let us go on to maturity."* These people had failed to meet that goal. They had become bored, dull and disinterested. They had become bogged down with things which, though true and important in themselves, were intended to be stepping stones to a deeper relationship with Christ. Many people confuse maturity with knowledge. They feel that if they learn enough about the Bible, they will be mature. That is how it should be but it does not always work out that way. The reason for this is that they trust in their knowledge instead of in the one to whom their knowledge should point. Spiritual maturity is not a case of becoming stronger and stronger. It involves becoming more and more dependent. Unless our knowledge makes us see our total weakness and helplessness outside Christ, it is a waste of time. Spiritually mature persons have come to the place in their lives where they are so aware, so convinced, of their own inadequacy that they are willing to trust the Lord completely, through all circumstances of life, no matter how dark or perplexing they may be. Corrie Ten Boom demonstrated spiritual maturity in the concentration camp. Hudson Taylor demonstrated it in China, and George Mueller in his Bristol orphanage. They did not strive for their own way, nor try to solve their problems in their own strength. They quietly trusted God to work out the details – and He did! That is spiritual maturity.

These Hebrew Christians were hitting political and social difficulties. Their faith was being tested. The going was getting tough. Their need was a growing faith, in which they developed dependence upon Christ. However, the enemy had side-tracked them. They were focusing on elementary points of doctrine, which, though true, would not help them when the sun got hot. A few examples are given in verses 1 and 2. They were not intended to be ends in themselves, but rather foundations upon which to build their faith. If someone were to set out to build a house but then liked the foundations so much that he stopped building, he would get very wet when it rained! Foundations are essential, but they are only the beginning of the project.

Verse 3:

"And this we will do if God permits."

This was the writer's stated goal – leaving the elemental doctrines and moving on toward a greater understanding of Christ Himself. This whole letter is about the ministry of Christ to the believer and His sufficiency on the believer's behalf.

Verses 4-6:

"For it is impossible for those who were once enlightened, and have tasted the heavenly gift, and have become partakers of the Holy Spirit, 5 and have tasted the good word of God and the powers of the age to come, 6 if they fall away, to renew them again to

repentance, since they crucify again for themselves the Son of God, and put Him to an open shame."

Here is one of the most controversial passages in the entire Bible. What shall we make of it? There are many different interpretations; prominent scholars can be found to support each point of view. Some say the passage teaches that if believers fall away, they lose their salvation and cannot be restored. Others claim that these were a special category of Christian and their danger of returning to Judaism was unique. Still others maintain that the people described here were not Christians at all. They had come close to receiving Christ, but were in danger of returning to their old ways. Obviously these theories cannot all be correct because they contradict one another. The only way to discover the truth is to appeal to Scripture itself and ask, "What does the Bible say? What does this letter say about itself?"

If the first interpretation is correct, and believers who fall away lose their salvation and cannot be restored, then the Bible contradicts itself and cannot be trusted. More serious still, since the Bible is the inspired Word of God, then God Himself cannot be relied upon either! Obviously this is untrue. The Bible is consistent in its teaching that there is no shadow of turning with God, that His promises are irrevocable and His grace is sufficient to wash out the deepest stains. If salvation were earned by good behavior, it would be logical to suppose that we might lose it by failing to maintain the standard. But since salvation is based solely upon the merits of Jesus Christ, and since all sin (past, present and future) was paid for upon the cross, our goodness or badness does not enter into the equation at all. Therefore, based upon the testimony of Scripture, it becomes patently obvious that Hebrews 6:4-6 does not teach that we could lose our salvation. Where there seems to be a contradiction there is also always an explanation.

The second theory (that these people were unique and were subject to different conditions from those affecting subsequent generations) does not ring true either. Such a thesis would do violence to the very basis of salvation, which is that the blood of Christ atoned for all sin, from the beginning of mankind to the end. Jesus did not die for some people and not for others. "God so loved the *world* that He gave His only begotten Son." At the cross, He was "reconciling the *world* unto

Himself." He died for all mankind. He was the propitiation for all sin, *"not for ours only but also for the whole world."* To claim that these first century Christians could irrevocably lose their salvation, while others could not, would contradict the clear teaching of Scripture.

The third theory, which claims that these people were not true Christians, but were "almost persuaded," certainly applies in some cases. There are many who fall into that category. They get involved with the local church and enjoy the atmosphere of fellowship. They make friends and appreciate the social activities. They may even be stirred by the messages they hear or the songs they sing, but they never make a personal commitment to Jesus Christ. Then there comes a day when something goes wrong, or they have a difference with somebody in the church, and they are gone. Their end could be worse than their beginning because now they are hardened toward the message of the Gospel.

However, I am not satisfied that that is the true meaning of this passage. Hebrews 3:1 clearly addresses the letter to *"Holy brethren, partakers of the heavenly calling,"* and calls them to *"consider the Apostle and High Priest of their confession.".* That sounds like full salvation. Also, in Hebrews 6:9 (immediately following the paragraph we are discussing) we read: *"But beloved, we are persuaded better things of you, and things that accompany salvation, though we thus speak."* Certainly, the writer accuses them of becoming dull of hearing, and of being babes when they should be teachers, but that confirms their salvation rather than casting doubt upon it. As we have seen, their danger was that of losing their rewards rather than their salvation.

A variation of this opinion is submitted by R.B. Theime, who points out correctly that the word translated *"since"*, or *"seeing"*, in verse 6 (*"since (seeing) they crucify again for themselves the Son of God, and put Him to an open shame"*) also means *"while."* This would change the meaning of the phrase. It would now read: "it is impossible to renew them to repentance *while*, (by their behavior), they crucify to themselves the Lord afresh and put Him to an open shame." I have discovered that to be true. Genuine Christians, who have grown cold in their faith, become almost impossible to reason with because they "know all the answers." Only a movement of the Holy Spirit will bring them back to their senses.

I remember a very successful pastor, many years ago, who enjoyed a fruitful ministry for a prolonged period of time. Then one day he ran away with his secretary and dropped out of the ministry. He knew the Bible well and though we had been his colleagues, we were unable to reach him with Scripture. It was *"impossible to renew him to repentance while he crucified the Lord afresh and put Him to an open shame."*

In addition to these views, there are actually indications that the writer to the Hebrews had a different focus in view. In this paragraph, he switches from the direct *"you"* to a hypothetical *"they"* (verse 6). He does not say, "If *you* fall away", he says "If *they* fall away it is impossible to renew *them*." First, these hypothetical persons were *"enlightened."* The word is in the passive voice, meaning that the enlightenment happened to them from outside themselves. God penetrated the darkness of their minds with His light. Second, they *"tasted"* of the heavenly gift. This is in the middle voice, which speaks of a person exercising his responsibility to respond to the light he has been given. Third, these hypothetical persons are *"partakers of the Holy Ghost."* Once again, that is passive, indicating that the action happened to them from outside. It is something God did. Fourth and fifth (verse 5) these people have *"tasted of the Word of God and the powers of the world to come."* The middle voice again pictures man meeting his responsibility to respond to the Spirit's promptings. That all paints a picture of salvation.

So far we have seen three things: First, that this passage cannot teach that a Christian could lose his salvation, second, that Christ would not apply different rules to different people, and third, that the writer to the Hebrews was obviously referring to people who were genuinely saved. However, we have also established that he is painting a hypothetical picture. He is not saying *"you;"* he is saying *"they."* Dr. Zodhiates claims that this is a teaching tool, designed to impress truth upon his readers. The original readers were experiencing difficult times. Their faith was under attack and some of them were wavering. Maybe some were asking questions: "Did we make a mistake in leaving the security of Judaism?" Doubt is a weapon which the enemy uses to great effect. So the writer paints a hypothetical picture for his readers. They have become dull of hearing and have lost their perspective. They cannot see the wood for the trees.

The writer says, in effect, "Suppose it were possible for someone who has seen the light, responded to it, received the Holy Spirit and become acquainted with the marvels of God's Word, to fall away and reject Jesus Christ. What then? Where would he turn for salvation? His works would not save him. Judaism would not save him. There is no salvation outside Christ. If he rejects the work which Jesus did historically on his behalf, and upon which his first repentance was based, his second repentance would have to be based on something else. The words translated "*renew again to repentance*" support this view. They indicate a new kind of repentance. What would this demand? It would require that Christ die all over again and be put to an open shame a second time in order to save him. That notion, of course, is absurd – and was intended to be absurd in order to prove a point. They already had the only salvation available to man. It was vested in the victory of Jesus Christ, who died, once for all, to atone for their sin. If they were to reject what they already had, there would be nowhere else to turn.

Verse 7:

"For the earth which drinks in the rain that often comes upon it, and bears herbs useful for those by whom it is cultivated, receives blessing from God;"

We all know that dry, parched land does not grow much fruit. Regardless of the reason, where water fails to reach the soil production is either stunted or non-existent. The Scriptures tell us that we are God's garden. He sows the seeds of faith in our hearts and then waters them by His Holy Spirit. In the Hebrews' case, something had caused their hearts to become dry and unproductive. The "water" of the Holy Spirit had been hindered in some way from reaching their hearts and refreshing the seed which God had planted there. Maybe something had grown up to obstruct it or something had been placed there to create a barrier. Whatever the reason, the people's hearts had become dry and they had grown "dull of hearing." They needed some husbandry to get them going again.

Verse 8:

"but if it bears thorns and briars, it is rejected and near to being cursed, whose end is to be burned."

It is an unfortunate fact that gardens grow weeds. Thorns and brambles seem to be happy anywhere, and under any conditions. Only the good things seem to die when water is denied them, and that is true spiritually as well. The only thing you can do with weeds in your flower bed is root them out and burn them. You don't burn the soil, of course. That remains the same. Similarly, in 1 Corinthians 3, where the judgment seat of Christ is described, it is not the Christian that is discarded, but useless works which are called "hay, wood and stubble." They are burned up because they are no use to God, but the Christian himself is saved. Here, the writer is saying the same thing. The believer is not in danger of being burned up, but his worldly ways are. However, the writer is not condemning his readers as worthless. . .

Verses 9-10:

"But, beloved, we are confident of better things concerning you, yes, things that accompany salvation, though we speak in this manner. 10 For God is not unjust to forget your work and labor of love which you have shown toward His name, in that you have ministered to the saints, and do minister."

Though accused of being "dull of hearing", these believers were still active. They were busy doing things that "accompany salvation." They were concerned for their fellow Christians and God was fully aware of their activities. It was not that they had given up their faith but that their hearts had become dry. It is very easy to slip into this condition. Many Christians continue to be active. They teach Sunday school, help in the nursery, sing in the choir, work as ushers, but their activities become routine and unrewarding. The joy has gone out of their service and worship. They do what they do more as a duty than as an act of love. Consequently, a burn-out becomes a real possibility. They become tired, even resentful, because there is not enough refreshment flowing into their hearts to keep them sweet. They are serving in their own strength, running on their own batteries, and sooner or later they become exhausted.

I was using a cordless screwdriver the other day and forgot to put it back on the charger. Next time I used it it lacked power and before the day was over it had packed up altogether. You can draw out without putting back in for a limited period but it is only a matter of time before exhaustion overtakes you

So the writer to the Hebrews challenges his readers and encourages them to look up and begin living again.

Verses 11-12:

"And we desire that each one of you show the same diligence to the full assurance of hope until the end, 12 that you do not become sluggish, but imitate those who through faith and patience inherit the promises."

There are fifteen references to "the promises" in Hebrews, six of which are in the eleventh chapter, where faith is stressed. Basically, promises and faith go hand in hand. A promise is not much use unless the one to whom the promise is made believes it. In order to believe it, certain conditions must be in place. For instance, the integrity of the promise-maker has to be reliable, and the ability of the promise-maker to carry out his promise must be beyond doubt. For instance, I don't trust some of the promises made by advertisers because, first, I don't know the persons making them and second, I doubt the truthfulness of the claims being made.

The Christian faith is founded on promises. Take the promises away and nothing would be left. The difference is that these promises are made by God, whose integrity is impeccable and whose ability to perform what He has promised is beyond question. Peter wrote in His first letter: *"God has given us great and precious promises, that **by these** we might be partakers of the divine nature."* Just think of that for a moment. You and I may be partakers of the divine nature by simply believing the promises and placing our confidence upon them. That is incredible! Salvation itself is a promise which must be believed before it is activated.

The indwelling Holy Spirit is the fulfillment of a promise. The coming resurrection is a promise and so is Heaven itself.

In this world, a treasury note is a promise. It is backed by the full faith and credit of the United States government. The only problem is that the ability of the government to cover its financial responsibilities is rapidly diminishing. By contrast, *these* "great and precious promises" are backed by the full faith and credit of Almighty God! His ability to guarantee His responsibilities will never be in question. He is *"the same, yesterday, today and forever."*

These Hebrew Christians must have believed the promises originally, or they would not have been Christians. But promises are intangible. You can't see or touch them. You have to keep them before your spiritual eyes and claim them daily by faith. Circumstances, on the other hand, thrust themselves upon our senses, without any effort on our part. We feel and experience them. They are the environment in which we live our lives. It is therefore very easy to allow them to take over. Peter did that when he walked on the water. He allowed the wind and the waves to overcome his faith and he sank. Evidently these people were in danger of doing the same, spiritually. As time went on they had allowed their circumstances to take precedence over their faith, and as the result their trust in God's promises had faded.

Back in chapter 5, verse 14, the writer refers to those who *"by reason of use had their senses exercised to discern good and evil."* The best possible exercise is that of reminding ourselves constantly of the great and precious promises upon which our faith is founded. Once we slack off with this exercise, our Christian walk ceases to have direction. There is nothing to keep it focused.

God's oath

Verses 13-15:

"For when God made a promise to Abraham, because He could swear by no one greater, He swore by Himself, 14 saying, "Surely blessing I will bless you, and multiplying I will multiply you." 15 And so, after he had patiently endured, he obtained the promise."

There was actually no need for God to swear at all, was there? He was under no obligation to prove anything to Abraham. God was God, and Abraham was but His creation. But in His grace, God stooped to Abraham's weakness and confirmed His promise with an oath. In consequence, Abraham believed God, and it was accounted unto him for righteousness. He "*patiently endured*," that is, he waited into his old age believing God would do what He had promised, and eventually He did. The key is "*patiently endured*." When God makes a promise it is absolutely reliable, but He rarely puts a time limit on it. We have to wait patiently for its fulfillment, and sometimes the waiting can be tough. Abraham waited and waited. His circumstances certainly did not encourage him but he kept on anyway. Throughout those weary years of waiting, God's spoken promise was all he had to support him. He had no document to read, no tape recording to play, no witness to confirm what he had heard. He had nothing but the promise of God in his memory, but he kept on believing, and eventually the promise was fulfilled, because it was guaranteed by the integrity of God's person.

Here, the sense is that we must follow Abraham's example. Unlike him, we *do* have God's promises in writing. We should treasure them, search them and know them. Our faith is based upon them, and by them, we "*become partakers of the divine nature.*"

Verse 16:

"*For men indeed swear by the greater, and an oath for confirmation is for them an end of all dispute.*"

An oath *should* be the end of all dispute, but unfortunately that is not always the case. However, men do not swear by someone or something weaker than themselves. They usually put their hand on the Bible and call upon God to be the witness. There is no greater power to which they can appeal. In a court of law, the oath seals the matter and the witness is assumed to be telling the truth. Anyone caught violating that trust is charged with perjury and can face serious consequences. Society, generally, accepts a sworn oath as the truth.

Verse 17:

"Thus God, determining to show more abundantly to the heirs of promise the immutability of His counsel, confirmed it by an oath."

To confirm the picture, first, God promised. He said, *"I will multiply your descendents as the stars of heaven and as the sand that is on the seashore; and your descendents shall possess the gate of their enemies, and in your seed shall all the nations of the earth be blessed."* The promise was immutable because God made it personally and He could not deny Himself. Then, twenty-five years later, God confirmed the promise with an oath. He said, *"Surely blessing I will bless you, and multiplying I will multiply you."* It was an irrevocable confirmation of the promise He had made to Abraham a quarter of a century previously.

Galatians 3 makes it clear that Jesus Christ is "Abraham's seed," and that you and I were made heirs of the promise when we trusted Christ for salvation. This clarified in the next verse:

Verse 18:

"That by two immutable things, in which it is impossible for God to lie, we might have strong consolation, who have fled for refuge to lay hold of the hope set before us."

"The hope set before us" is, of course, the promise of eternal glory in the presence of the Lord. By trusting Christ, we *"flee for refuge"* from the judgment that has been pronounced upon all men. There are illustrations of this in the Old Testament. In those days there were "cities of refuge", to which a person who had unintentionally killed someone could flee for safety. Once inside, they were secure from those who would do them harm. Then in 1 Kings we read about two separate individuals (Adonijah and Joab) who fled to the tabernacle and laid hold of the horns of the altar. The idea was the same. They sought refuge there. In God's house they felt safe from the wrath which threatened them. This verse carries the same sense. The wrath of God abides upon all men because of their sin, but we are exhorted to *"flee for refuge"* and to lay hold, not on the horns of the altar, but upon *"the hope that is set before us."*

What hope? The hope of John 3:16, which promises eternal life to all who believe; the hope of John 10:27-29, which says that those who trust Christ shall never perish, and the hope of 1 Corinthians 15:51-54, which promises that these corruptible bodies will one day be exchanged for bodies that are incorruptible, and death will be swallowed up in victory. That is the hope we are to lay hold of. The next verses clarify it further.

The anchor of the soul

Verses 19-20:

> *"This hope we have as an anchor of the soul, both sure and steadfast, and which enters the Presence behind the veil, 20 where the forerunner has entered for us, even Jesus, having become High Priest forever according to the order of Melchizedek."*

An anchor gives stability. It extends (in physical terms) to the bottom of the sea and grips the rock on behalf of the ship. It is an extension of the ship itself. It is an arm which connects an unstable and wave-tossed ship to the stable and unaffected sea floor. Down there all is peace. The wind doesn't blow, the waves do not roar and the ship is connected to that peace and security, even in the midst of the storm. In the spiritual sense, the promises of God provide an anchor to the soul, which extends, not to the sea floor but to a place within the veil – the holy of holies in Heaven – where the presence of God resides. The soul's anchor connects him or her to God's holy of holies. Jesus (our Forerunner) took it there as our high priest. In that place is "the peace of God which passes all understanding." The believer is connected by the anchor of faith to the promises of God, and no matter how fiercely the storms of life may rage, the anchor (sure and steadfast) will hold the soul secure.

At this point, the "detour" that began in chapter 5, verse 10 comes to an end and we are brought back to the main highway of teaching. The final words of verse 20 supply the connecting link: *"even Jesus, made a high priest forever, after the order of Melchisedek."* When he reached this point in chapter 5, the writer broke off and explained that his readers were unable to understand deep spiritual things because they had become "dull of hearing." He then explained how they could regain their powers of discernment. The difficult subject to which he referred concerned the mysterious Melchisedek, which he takes the whole of chapter 7 to explain.

CHAPTER 7

Melchizedek again

Due to the descriptive nature of this chapter, multiple verses are selected for comment, rather than single verses as in previous chapters. That being so, we shall move fairly quickly through the section.

Verses 1-3:

"For this Melchizedek, king of Salem, priest of the Most High God, who met Abraham returning from the slaughter of the kings and blessed him, 2 to whom also Abraham gave a tenth part of all, first being translated "king of righteousness," and then also king of Salem, meaning "king of peace," 3 without father, without mother, without genealogy, having neither beginning of days nor end of life, but made like the Son of God, remains a priest continually."

The central sentence in this passage begins with the first three words of verse 1 and ends with the last four of verse 3. *"For this Melchisedek. . . . .remains a priest continually."* The words in between describe the nature of this mysterious person, and help us grasp how very different from other men he was.

In Genesis 14, a confederacy of kings attacked Sodom, where Lot (Abram's nephew) lived. They carried off Lot, together with many others, and plundered their goods. When Abram heard the news, he armed his servants, gave chase to the departing invaders and destroyed them, rescuing the people and their goods and bringing back considerable extra spoils which had belonged to the attacking kings. As Abram returned, he was met by Melchisedek, who blessed him and said, *"Blessed be Abram of God most high, possessor of Heaven and earth."* In return, Abram gave Melchisedek a tithe, or tenth, of all the spoils. We are not told in the Scriptures where Melchisedek came from, who he was or where he went.

135 years before Christ, Rabbi Ismael considered him to be Shem, Noah's son. Martin Luther and others accepted his view. Others claimed that he was the archangel, Michael. Some go so far as to say he was Christ Himself. But the fact remains that nobody knows. The Scriptures do not tell us. It seems to me that if God wanted us to know his identity He would have told us.

The important thing is that Melchisedek was clearly a type of Christ. The passage in Hebrews gives us more details than the Genesis account. It states that Melchisedek was, by interpretation, *"King of Righteousness"*, *King of Salem* (which means "King of Peace") and *"priest of the most high God."* He did not come from any of the tribes of Israel, because he lived long before Israel (Jacob) was born. Perhaps the most striking thing about him was that, unlike most prominent Hebrews of antiquity, his genealogy was missing. Verse 3 says, in effect, "We don't know who his father was, or his mother; we don't know where he was born, or when he died. He seemed to be timeless, more like a son of God than a son of man. It was as though he had always been a priest, and always would be."

Then verses 4-7 continue:

> *"Now consider how great this man was, to whom even the patriarch Abraham gave a tenth of the spoils. 5 And indeed those who are of the sons of Levi, who receive the priesthood, have a commandment to receive tithes from the people according to the law, that is, from their brethren, though they have come from the loins of Abraham; 6 but he whose genealogy is not derived from them received tithes from Abraham and blessed him who had the promises. 7 Now beyond all contradiction the lesser is blessed by the better.*

What does all that mean? The reasoning is simple enough. It is simply that Melchisedek had to be great because he blessed Abram, who was the founder of the nation, and in response Abram gave him tithes. Aaron, from whom the priesthood of Israel later descended, had not yet been born. His genes still resided within Abram's body. Aaron and his descendents (the tribe of Levi) from which Aaron eventually came, were commanded by God to *receive* tithes from the people, but symbolically they *paid* tithes to Melchisedek in Abram, because their genes resided within him. That made Melchisedek greater than them all.

Verses 8-10:

"Here mortal men receive tithes, but there he receives them, of whom it is witnessed that he lives. 9 Even Levi, who receives tithes, paid tithes through Abraham, so to speak, 10 for he was still in the loins of his father when Melchizedek met him."

That simply restates what we have already discussed.

Verse 11:

"Therefore, if perfection were through the Levitical priesthood (for under it the people received the law), what further need was there that another priest should rise according to the order of Melchizedek, and not be called according to the order of Aaron?"

Why indeed? Remember, the original readers of this letter were Christians who had become discouraged. They were thinking of slipping back to the old system of Levitical priests. Now they were confronted by a question: If the Levitical priesthood was so good, why was Christ proclaimed by God to be *"a priest for ever after the order of Melchisedek?"*

Verses 12-14:

"For the priesthood being changed, of necessity there is also a change of the law. 13 For He of whom these things are spoken belongs to another tribe, from which no man has officiated at the altar. 14 For it is evident that our Lord arose from Judah, of which tribe Moses spoke nothing concerning priesthood."

Under Old Testament law, the priesthood was confined to the tribe of Levi. Nobody from any other tribe was allowed to officiate. Jesus, however, came from the tribe of Judah, not Levi, and by proclaiming Him *"a priest forever,"* God clearly set the old law aside. That being so, what point was there in these people returning to it?

Verses 15-17:

"And it is yet far more evident if, in the likeness of Melchizedek, there arises another priest 16 who has come, not according to the law of a fleshly commandment, but according to the power of an endless life. 17 For He testifies: "You are a priest forever according to the order of Melchizedek.""

From Aaron (the first priest) down, every priest grew old and eventually died. There were no exceptions. But here was a priest who would never die. That evidence was even greater than the switch from Levi to Judah.

Verses 18-19:

"For on the one hand there is an annulling of the former commandment because of its weakness and unprofitableness, 19 for the law made nothing perfect; on the other hand, there is the bringing in of a better hope, through which we draw near to God."

Here we are back to hope again, but this was a "better hope". It out-dates and supersedes the old law, with its temporary priesthood and symbolic sacrifices. The old Law of Moses made nothing perfect. It pointed out the way things ought to be but offered no assistance in meeting its standard. This new hope was better, enabling sinful men to draw closer to God. This hope is seen to be the Lord Jesus Himself.

Verses 20-22:

"And inasmuch as He was not made priest without an oath 21 (for they have become priests without an oath, but He with an oath by Him who said to Him: "The Lord has sworn and will not relent, 'You are a priest forever according to the order of Melchizedek' ") 22 by so much more Jesus has become a surety of a better covenant."

The Old Testament priests were appointed because of their bloodline. They inherited the priesthood. By contrast, Jesus was appointed by God Himself, who did it with an oath (which we have seen several times in this passage). Thus, the Old covenant was replaced by a new covenant and Jesus Himself became its surety or guarantor.

Verses 23-25:

"And there were many priests, because they were prevented by death from continuing. 24 But He, because He continues forever, has an unchangeable priesthood. 25 Therefore He is also able to save to the uttermost those who come to God through Him, since He ever lives to make intercession for them."

From Aaron onwards, Levitical priests were born and died. Their term of office was limited by the natural ravages of time upon their mortal bodies. But this man, Jesus, was not mortal. He was not affected by time. He is a priest forever. He belongs to a new order and is therefore able to *"save to the uttermost those who come to God through Him."* He ever lives to make intercession for them.

Verses 26-28:

"For such a High Priest was fitting for us, who is holy, harmless, undefiled, separate from sinners, and has become higher than the heavens; 27 who does not need daily, as those high priests, to offer up sacrifices, first for His own sins and then for the people's, for this He did once for all when He offered up Himself. 28 For the law appoints as high priests men who have weakness, but the word of the oath, which came after the law, appoints the Son who has been consecrated forever."

What a wonderful commentary! Just think of it -- we have a great high priest representing us, who is so far above any other priest who ever lived that there is no comparison. He belongs to a new order; he is the guarantor of a new covenant; He is appointed by God; He is holy, harmless, undefiled, separate from sinners and made higher than the heavens. He is eternal and ever lives to intercede for us before the throne of God! Why would anyone even contemplate turning away and going back to the old system?

Who in their right mind would consider returning to the old covenant, with its mortal priests who were sinners by nature like everybody else, and to the continual burnt offerings, which were only symbols of the real thing? The only possible reason was that the original readers of this letter did not fully understand what they had in Christ. It is still the same today. The greatest need is still for Christians to grasp the true nature of the salvation they have been given.

This is a heavy chapter but it is of enormous importance. The devil would have us skip over it. He would tell us that it refers exclusively to ancient Jewish society and has no bearing on our lives today. But that is not true. This chapter contains the material that the writer wanted to explain back in chapter 5 but felt his readers were not yet ready to receive it. He wanted them to understand that outside Christ there was no-one and no-thing that could save them, or represent them before God. The old covenant had been set aside, together with its priesthood and sacrifices, and a new covenant had taken its place. There was now only one priest and one sacrifice, both of which are eternal.

"For there in one God and one mediator between God and men, the man Christ Jesus." (1 Timothy 2:5)

CHAPTER 8

Summary

This chapter is largely a summary of the previous material. The opening statement makes this clear.

Verse 1:

"Now this is the sum of the things we are saying:"

First, *"We have such a High Priest, who is seated at the right hand of the throne of the Majesty in the heavens."*

That is where He ministers. He is not here on earth (like human priests are). He is at the right hand of God Himself.

Second (verse 2): He is *"a Minister of the sanctuary and of the true tabernacle which the Lord erected, and not man."*

Whether or not there is an actual tabernacle in Heaven is not known for certain, but we do know that the throne of God is there and that the Lord Jesus is ever present to intercede for us.

Third (verse 3): *"For every high priest is appointed to offer both gifts and sacrifices. Therefore it is necessary that this One also have something to offer."*

Verse 4:

"For if He were on earth, He would not be a priest, since there are priests who offer the gifts according to the law."

Our great High Priest in Heaven is different from the priests on earth because the priests of Israel all came from the family of Levi, whereas Jesus came through the tribe of Judah. There was no need for a different type of priest on earth because the priests of Israel offered up all the sacrifices required by God's law. Therefore this heavenly priest must have a greater, higher ministry than they had. Question: How did the earthly priests minister?

Answer, Verses 5:

"They serve the example and shadow of the heavenly things, as Moses was divinely instructed when he was about to make the tabernacle. For He said, "See that you make all things according to the pattern shown you on the mountain."

The Levitical priests merely served the example and shadow of the real thing. The "real thing" was, of course, the Person and ministry of the Lord Jesus. God gave Moses specific instructions to build an earthly tabernacle, and every part of it spoke of some aspect of the great High Priest who would one day come. The earthly priests did not understand this but they went about their duties as they were commanded. In doing so, they served the shadow of the real thing.

Verses 6-7:

"But now He has obtained a more excellent ministry, inasmuch as He is also Mediator of a better covenant, which was established on better promises. 7 For if that first covenant had been faultless, then no place would have been sought for a second."

That is logical. Why introduce a new law if the old one met the need? In fact, the old law did not meet the need. The need of mankind was salvation, and, as Paul wrote in Romans 3:19,*"By the works of the law can no flesh be justified."* The law failed because it told man how he should live but offered him no help in fulfilling its conditions. Instead of saving him, it condemned him.

Back in Genesis 14, over four centuries before the law was given, God appeared to Abraham and made him three promises. Perhaps it would be more accurate to say that He gave Abraham one promise in three parts. The *first* had to do with the *land*, which God said He would give to Abraham's descendents; the *second* concerned the *nation*, which God said He would raise up from Abraham's descendents, and the *third* concerned the *blessing*, which God said would come upon all nations of the world through Abraham's seed.

Throughout the following centuries it was assumed that this last part of the promise simply meant that the nation which sprang from Abraham would, in some way, be a blessing to the whole world. It has been. To begin with, Israel gave us the Bible. The prophets, psalmists and historians of the Old Testament all came from Israel. Most important of all, Israel gave us the Lord Jesus Christ. He came as Israel's promised Messiah, but when He died He paid for the sins of the whole world.

However, Jesus could not redeem sinful man under the old covenant because the old covenant demanded a standard which nobody could meet. He therefore replaced the old covenant with a new one. Here in verse 8 the writer shows how God promised the new covenant, through the prophet Jeremiah, 600 years before Christ was born. Quoting Jeremiah 31:31-34, he writes:

Verses 8-10:

"Because finding fault with them, He says: "Behold, the days are coming," says the Lord, "when I will make a new covenant with the house of Israel and with the house of Judah: 9 not according to the covenant that I made with their fathers in the day when I took them by the hand to lead them out of the land of Egypt; because they did not continue in My covenant, and I disregarded them, says the Lord. 10 For this is the covenant that I will make with the house of Israel: After those days, says the Lord, I will put My laws in their mind and write them on their hearts; and I will be their God, and they shall be My people."

That was the New Covenant (or, as we say today, "The New Testament.") This has now been fulfilled in Christ. The sign of the Old Testament was circumcision, which symbolized holiness to the Lord. The sign of the New Testament is the wine of the communion service, which symbolizes the shed blood of the ultimate sacrifice.

The differences between the two covenants are fundamental. For instance, under the New Testament, we may now go directly to God through Christ. Human mediators are forever set aside. We can pray for one another, teach one another and exhort one another, but there is only one priest through whom we can approach God. That is the Lord Jesus.

Another important difference is the "*inwardness*" of the New Covenant. The church, as we know it today, was born in Acts chapter 2, when the Holy Spirit fell on the assembled disciples. Instantly, they were changed and empowered from inside. This could not have happened before Christ died. The Holy Spirit was free to indwell these people only because their sin had been cancelled on the cross. He could not have come under any other condition. As it was, His presence among them brought with it a desire and a motivation to do God's will, together with the ability to do it. It was an inward thing, and today the process is still the same.

Verses 11-12:

"None of them shall teach his neighbor, and none his brother, saying, 'Know the Lord,' for all shall know me, from the least of them to the greatest of them. 12 For I will be merciful to their unrighteousness, and their sins and their lawless deeds I will remember no more."

This passage can be easily misunderstood. It does not infer that there would no longer be Bible teachers under the New Covenant. One of the spiritual gifts endowed by the Holy Spirit is the gift of teaching, and the New Testament letters, including this one, are all designed to teach. Pastor-teachers are specifically listed in Ephesians 4:11 among the gifted personnel God has given to the church and one of the qualifications of elders is that they should be "*apt to teach*."

However, the best human teacher in the world is unable to impart spiritual truth to the heart of another individual. Only the Holy Spirit can do that. When I first entered the ministry I used to think to myself, "*If only I could make the Gospel just a little clearer, people would understand and be saved.*" I would therefore struggle over every word in an effort to reach more people. But as I grew in my faith I came to realize that souls are not saved through logic. They can be saved only by the agency of the Holy Spirit. No matter how clear I made the message, unless the Lord drew people to Himself I was simply spinning my wheels. It is not in our power to *persuade* men and women to trust Christ. That is God's job, not the teacher's.

One of the greatest characteristics of the New Covenant is that God speaks to individuals personally and draws them to Himself. The disciples knew the Scriptures well but it was not until Jesus taught them on the road to Emmaus that their spiritual eyes were opened. That is how it still works today. The only real teacher of spiritual things is the Lord. He uses human agency but only as a vehicle for His Spirit.

Having summarized chapter 7, the writer now draws a conclusion.

Verse 13:

"In that He says, "A new covenant," He has made the first obsolete. Now what is becoming obsolete and growing old is ready to vanish away."

The old Law of Moses, with its mortal priests and symbolic sacrifices, simply pointed the way to a new system, in which there is one eternal priest and one eternal sacrifice. The new system had now been inaugurated, the eternal sacrifice had been made and the eternal priest installed. That rendered the old law obsolete.

CHAPTER 9

The Old Covenant

As in many other places in the New Testament, we may ignore the chapter division and move right into chapter 9, where the same line of reasoning continues.

The first seven verses describe the tabernacle that Moses made. It was comprised of two rooms, or compartments. In the first room (called the Sanctuary) stood the lampstand, the altar of incense and the table of showbread. This was where the priests ministered. A veil separated the two rooms and behind the veil were the golden censor, the Ark of the Covenant (overlaid with gold) and the two cherubim overshadowing the mercy seat. Inside the Ark were three articles, which spoke of God's provision and sovereignty. These were a golden pot, containing one day's ration of manna from the wilderness, Aaron's rod, which budded, blossomed and bore fruit overnight to endorse his appointment to the priesthood, and the two tablets of stone upon which the finger of God had traced the Ten Commandments. This second room was called "The Holiest of All" (The Holy of Holies) and only the High Priest was allowed to enter it. Once each year, he passed behind the veil and entered the Holy of Holies, carrying the blood of the sacrifice, to atone for his own sin and for the sins of the people.

The text is fairly straightforward.

Verses 1-7:

"Then indeed, even the first covenant had ordinances of divine service and the earthly sanctuary. 2 For a tabernacle was prepared: the first part, in which was the lamp stand, the table, and the showbread, which is called the sanctuary; 3 and behind the second

veil, the part of the tabernacle which is called the Holiest of All, 4 which had the golden altar of incense and the ark of the covenant overlaid on all sides with gold, in which were the golden pot that had the manna, Aaron's rod that budded, and the tablets of the covenant; 5 and above it were the cherubim of glory overshadowing the mercy seat. Of these things we cannot now speak in detail. 6 Now when these things had been thus prepared, the priests always went into the first part of the tabernacle, performing the services. 7 But into the second part the high priest went alone once a year, not without blood, which he offered for himself and for the people's sins committed in ignorance."

Verses 8-10:

"The Holy Spirit indicating this, that the way into the Holiest of All was not yet made manifest while the first tabernacle was still standing. 9 It was symbolic for the present time in which both gifts and sacrifices are offered which cannot make him who performed the service perfect in regard to the conscience - 10 concerned only with foods and drinks, various washings, and fleshly ordinances imposed until the time of reformation."

Under the Old Covenant, the way into the Holy of Holies had not yet been opened. An impenetrable barrier stood between the people and God. The veil represented this barrier and nobody dare violate it. The priests ministered daily in the outer room and the High Priest entered once per year into the inner room, but nothing they did could wash the conscience clean. Their ministry was just a ceremony, like all the other ceremonies, which symbolized the ultimate atonement that would come one day on the future.

Verses 1-10 describe the earthly tabernacle and the worship that took place within it. The original readers of this letter would have had no problem following along because they were very familiar with what the writer described. However, he had a purpose for his reminder. He was now going to contrast the ministry of the earthly priests with that of the heavenly priest and to demonstrate the heavenly priest's superiority over everything they had known.

Verses 11- 14:

"But Christ came as High Priest of the good things to come, with the greater and more perfect tabernacle not made with hands, that is, not of this creation. 12 Not with the blood of goats and calves, but with His own blood He entered the Most Holy Place once for all, having obtained eternal redemption. 13 For if the blood of bulls and goats and the ashes of a heifer, sprinkling the unclean, sanctifies for the purifying of the flesh, 14 how much more shall the blood of Christ, who through the eternal Spirit offered Himself without spot to God, purge your conscience from dead works to serve the living God?"

During all those years under the Old Covenant, the priests had been unconsciously playing out a story. It has been written before the world began, but no-one had understood it. *"Eye had not seen, nor ear heard, neither had it entered into the heart of man, the things which God had prepared for those who loved Him."* But suddenly it *had* been revealed by the Holy Spirit. Suddenly the story which had been acted out so often, first in the tabernacle and later in the temple, made sense. When Jesus died, the veil of the temple was torn in two from the top to the bottom. The way into the Holy of Holies was dramatically opened up. Of course, the barrier which had kept man separated from God for so many years was not actually the veil, but sin. No matter how many animals died; no matter how many times the priests ministered, the problem of sin remained, until one day a lonely figure was nailed to a cross and the sins of the world were laid upon Him. On that day, one who had known no sin was made to be sin in our place, and the barrier which had stood for so long between us was finally removed.

Never imagine that this barrier was frail or flimsy. The veil of the temple was made of woven tapestry, sixty feet high and four inches thick. Only the hand of God could have torn it in two, from the top to the bottom. It spoke eloquently of the barrier which sin had placed between man and God. Only God could have parted it. No human agency possessed the power to achieve such a feat. Similarly, only God could penetrate the barrier which kept man isolated from salvation before Jesus came. The awe with which the priests viewed the torn veil must have been beyond description.

Chapter 9

The New Covenant

Verse 15:

"And for this reason He is the Mediator of the new covenant, by means of death, for the redemption of the transgressions under the first covenant, that those who are called may receive the promise of the eternal inheritance."

The promise of the inheritance is the Holy Spirit Himself. In the Bible He is called *"The Holy Spirit of Promise."* In Ephesians 1, verse 11 tells us that by trusting in Christ we obtain an eternal inheritance, and verse 13 says that after we believe we are *"sealed with the Holy Spirit of Promise, who is the earnest of our inheritance until the redemption of the purchased possession."* The door was opened for Him to dwell within each believer because the blood of Christ was shed, once for all, to atone for sin.

Verse 16:

"For where there is a testament, there must also of necessity be the death of the testator."

A testament is a will. We speak today of making a *"last will and testament"* but wills are not much use until the persons making them have died.

Verses 17-22:

"For a testament is in force after men are dead, since it has no power at all while the testator lives. 18 Therefore not even the first covenant was dedicated without blood. 19 For when Moses had spoken every precept to all the people according to the law, he took the blood of calves and goats, with water, scarlet wool, and hyssop, and sprinkled both the book itself and all the people, 20 saying, "This is the blood of the covenant which God has commanded you." 21 Then likewise he sprinkled with blood both the tabernacle and all the vessels of the ministry. 22 And according to the law almost all things are purged with blood, and without shedding of blood there is no remission."

The people who first read this letter were well aware of the rules of justice. There could be no forgiveness without a penalty being paid, and the penalty for sin was death. Either the sinner, or something that would represent the sinner, had to die. Throughout the years of the Old Testament, animals stood in for the people. Innocent animals died and the guilty people went free. It was not fair by any means but that was the way it worked. Every time a lamb was offered as a sacrifice, it was a reminder that sin was the cause of its death – not its own sin, because it had none, but the sin of the person offering it.

Verses 23-24:

"Therefore it was necessary that the copies of the things in the heavens should be purified with these, but the heavenly things themselves with better sacrifices than these. 24 For Christ has not entered the holy places made with hands, which are copies of the true, but into heaven itself, now to appear in the presence of God for us."

In the prophetic words of John the Baptist, Jesus was *"The Lamb of God that takes away the sins of the world."* He inaugurated "a better covenant", won for us by a better sacrifice – a once for all settlement which satisfied justice to the full.

Verses 25-26:

"Not that He should offer Himself often, as the high priest enters the Most Holy Place every year with blood of another - 26 He then would have had to suffer often since the foundation of the world; but now, once at the end of the ages, He has appeared to put away sin by the sacrifice of Himself."

Earthly priests, who had no power to atone for sin, were obliged to offer animal sacrifices over and over again. Year after year the high priest went behind the veil with the blood of the sacrifice, to seek atonement for the people. This activity was merely a picture of what was to come. The priests played out a charade, so to speak, acting out the drama of the final sacrifice, which would one day come to pass. When Jesus died, his sacrifice was the real thing. When He said *"It is finished"* that is precisely what He meant. The play-acting was forever over; the work of redemption was complete; the price was paid, and the way opened for you and for me to receive eternal life. There was no need to repeat the sacrifice. When God the Son shed His blood, God the Father was satisfied. The price had been paid. There would never be anything else to do.

Verse 27:

"And as it is appointed for men to die once, but after this the judgment, 28 so Christ was offered once to bear the sins of many. To those who eagerly wait for Him He will appear a second time, apart from sin, for salvation."

Jesus is coming back one day, and when He does, sin will be a forgotten subject. For those who are trusting in His finished work, their sin has been removed as far as the east is from the west. Their record in Heaven no longer bears any witness to it. It is paid for and finished with. True, we shall all stand before the bema seat of Christ and receive or lose rewards according to our faithfulness in this life, but sin will not be mentioned. It is over and finished with.

It is a fact that every man and every woman must eventually die. Death is a fact of life which cannot be escaped. In the same way, Christ's atoning death is a fact. It stands as a mountain top in history and no power on earth or in heaven could cancel or change it. One day, the risen and victorious Lord will appear, not as a lowly carpenter but as King of kings and Lord of Lords.

CHAPTER 10

All believers are holy

God is holy. Holiness is one of His essential characteristics. He is holy because He is totally separated from anything unclean or impure. That is what *"holy"* means. When Peter wrote *"As He is holy, so be ye holy"* he did not expect his readers to be like God. That was not possible. He meant "separate yourselves from evil things, just as God is separated from them." God's Spirit is the Holy Spirit and when the angelic host ascribes praise to God they sing, *"Holy, holy, holy is the Lord God of Hosts."* He is above, beyond and apart from anything and anyone who is defiled.

In the Greek language, God is said to be *"hagios"* or sacred. For this reason it was necessary, in the days of the tabernacle and later, of the temple, to manifest Himself in a *"hagion"* or sanctuary (a place set apart from contamination by sinful man and closed off by a veil). However, because it was necessary for the priests to minister in the tabernacle and temple, and for the high priest to go behind the veil once per year on the Day of Atonement, these men had to be *"sanctified"* (made holy), and a person who has been made holy is called a *"saint."*

So now we have a string of words, all of which come from the same root and have to do with the act of being set apart for God's use, -- *"holy," "sacred," "sanctuary," "sanctified"* and *"saint."* And the opening passage of this chapter explains the way in which every believer has been sanctified and is therefore reckoned by God to be a saint.

Now there are several areas of the Christian faith which have two levels of operation. One level is that of our *position* in Christ, and the other is that of our *walk* here on earth. In each case, the first level is termed *"positional"* and the second level *"experiential."* Take peace, for example. *"Positional peace"* is something which has been won for us by Jesus Christ. At the cross, reconciliation was made between God and man. Hostilities came to an end and peace was established. Paul wrote in Romans 5:1, *"Therefore, having been justified by faith, we have peace with God through our Lord Jesus Christ."* That kind of peace is not necessarily something that you feel. You don't experience it. It is yours; every Christian has it, but you enter into it because of your position in Christ. You are at peace with God in the sense that He is no longer your judge but has become your Father and Friend.

However, the *feeling of peace* is also promised to those who trust the Lord. In Philippians 4:6-7 Paul writes: *"Be anxious for nothing, but in everything by prayer and supplication, with thanksgiving, let your requests be made known unto God, and the peace of God that passes all understanding shall keep your hearts and minds through Christ Jesus."* That is *felt* peace. The first kind is positional and the second is experiential.

Now sanctification is the same. There is positional sanctification, with which every Christian has been endowed, and there is experiential sanctification, which we are exhorted to pursue. This passage has to do with the first category. The first 10 verses of chapter 10 explain how the Old Testament religious system failed to deliver the goods.

Verses 1-2:

"For the law, having a shadow of the good things to come, and not the very image of the things, can never with these same sacrifices, which they offer continually year by year, make those who approach perfect. 2 For then would they not have ceased to be offered? For the worshipers, once purged, would have had no more consciousness of sins."

The very fact that they offered the same sacrifices over and over again proved that the offerings were ineffective. Had they achieved their purpose, they would have ceased. There would be no need to continually pay a bill that has already been settled. However, God ordained these sacrifices for a purpose.

Verses 3-4:

"But in those sacrifices there is a reminder of sins every year. 4 For it is not possible that the blood of bulls and goats could take away sins."

The Old Testament sacrifices served, not as an actual atonement for sin, but as a reminder of the sin itself. Every time a sacrifice was offered up, the people making it were reminded (in a very graphic way) that they were guilty, and that the penalty for sin was death. God designed the sacrificial system to point forward to a time in the future, when sin would be cancelled forever. The next verses describe the process whereby this final cancellation of sin took place.

We all know that Jesus died to pay the penalty for sin and that He was the fulfillment of all the Old Testament types. However, we also need to be reminded of it. We need to be continually confronted with the price of our salvation. If we are not reminded it is very easy to slip into a comfortable frame of mind in which we take our salvation for granted and forget that we were all guilty sinners, bound for hell, with no way to help ourselves until Christ stepped in and saved us. It would also be easy to forget that had it not been for Christ's atonement we would all still be irrevocably lost today. We must never lose sight of the fact that the salvation we enjoy was won for us by the suffering of somebody else, and the fact that the "somebody else" happened to God Himself makes the miracle infinitely more marvelous.

The final sacrifice

Now back to verse 5:

"Therefore, when He came into the world, He said: "Sacrifice and offering you did not desire, but a body you have prepared for Me."

The basis of that explanation is a quotation from Psalm 40. It is taken right out of the Septuagint version of the Old Testament. The Septuagint was a Greek translation of the Hebrew text, made about 200 years before the birth of Christ and used extensively by the early church. The Lord Jesus and Paul quoted from it frequently. If you were to read Psalm 40 in your present Bible, you would notice a difference between what you read there and what you see here in Hebrews 10. The reason for this is simply that the writer to the Hebrews was quoting from the old Greek translation, rather than from the later Hebrew.

The difference between the two Versions is interesting. In the Hebrew text, from which our Old Testament is taken, Psalm 40:6 reads: *"sacrifice and offering you did not desire; my ears have you opened."* Here, in verse 5, it is translated as *"sacrifice and offering you did not desire, but a body you have prepared for me."* The reason for the difference is unclear but both speak of the Messiah who would one day come, and both refer to the total obedience that would characterize His ministry and personality. Christ came specifically to do the will of the Father and this is spelled out in the next verses.

Verses 6-7:

"In burnt offerings and sacrifices for sin you had no pleasure. 7 Then I said, 'Behold, I have come - in the volume of the book it is written of me - to do your will, O God.' "

God, the Word, always existed. He inhabited eternity as an equal member of the Godhead. But there came a day when the eternal Word took human form and "became flesh." As Jesus, the Messiah, His one purpose was to fulfill the counsel of the Godhead concerning salvation. The testimony of Jesus Himself bears witness to this. Here are several verses that illustrate this fact:

John 4:34: *"My meat is to do the will of Him who sent me, and to finish the work."*

John 5:30: *"I seek not my own will, but the will of the Father who has sent me."*

John 6:38-40: *"I came down from Heaven, not to do my own will, but the will of Him who sent me. 39 And this is the will of the Father who sent me, that of all He has given me I should lose nothing, but should raise it up again at the last day. 40 And this is the will of Him who sent me that everyone who sees the Son, and*

believes on Him, may have everlasting life; and I will raise him up
on the last day."

Matthew, Mark and Luke all record that in the Garden of Gethsemane, when the terror of the cross loomed dark before Him, Jesus said, *"Nevertheless, not as I will but as thou wilt."*

So here in Hebrews 10, this truth is being spotlighted by using the prophetic words of David. God took no pleasure in burnt offerings and blood sacrifices. He said through the prophet, Samuel, 1,000 years before Christ was born, *"To obey is better than sacrifice, and to listen is better than the fat of rams."* Later, in Psalm 51, David prayed and said, *"You desire not sacrifice, else I would give it; you delight not in burnt offerings. The sacrifices of God are a broken spirit, a broken and a contrite heart."* Later still, the prophet Isaiah said to the people of his day, because of their hypocrisy: *"To what purpose is the multitude of your sacrifices to me? Says the Lord; I am full of burnt offerings of rams, and the fat of fed beasts; I delight not in the blood of bullocks, or of lambs or of he-goats."* God was more concerned with the condition of the people's hearts than with the offerings they brought. They imagined that by going through religious rituals they could satisfy God and keep Him happy. In fact, nothing could be further from the truth.

God has been accused of being a "bloody God" because He desired "all those sacrifices" but the sacrifices were never for God's pleasure. They were to impress upon the people making them that sin has terrible consequences. Sin kills, sin destroys, and the people needed to be reminded, over and over again, that they were guilty before God. So are we, of course. If man was ever to be saved from the consequences of his own sin, the sin itself had to be dealt with. Somehow, the unholy had to made holy; the sinner had to be sanctified, and since man was incapable of doing that for himself, someone else had to do it for him. As the hymn-write put it:

"There was no other good enough,
To pay the price of sin.
He only could unlock the gate
Of Heaven, and let us in."

Jesus did that by obedience to the Father's will.

Verses 8-9"

"Previously saying, "Sacrifice and offering, burnt offerings, and offerings for sin you did not desire, nor had pleasure in them" (which are offered according to the law), 9 then He said, "Behold, I have come to do your will, O God." He takes away the first that He may establish the second."

The first thing that was taken away was the system of sacrifices and the second thing, with which the first was replaced, was the offering of Jesus, which involved His total submission to the Father's will.

Verse 10:

"By that will we have been sanctified through the offering of the body of Jesus Christ once for all."

This refers to our *"positional sanctification."* In Christ, we are declared to be holy. Believers of all ages are forever set apart for God's use. It is not something that we do, or achieve, or feel. It is not a "second blessing." Sinners are declared to be saints as the result of Christ's sacrifice on the cross. He paid the debt and we are set free.

Verses 11-13:

"And every priest stands ministering daily and offering repeatedly the same sacrifices, which can never take away sins. 12 But this Man, after He had offered one sacrifice for sins forever, sat down at the right hand of God, 13 from that time waiting till His enemies are made His footstool."

As we have seen, the old sacrifices were repeated over and over again, day after day, year in, year out. But here was a once-for-all transaction which closed the account forever. It was so complete that Christ *"sat down"* at God's right hand. There was nothing left to do. The work was finished and the Savior could *"expect"* His enemies (Satan, his power of death, the rebellious angels and all those who rejected His offer of salvation) to be made His footstool. He would have final and complete victory over them.

Verse 14:

"For by one offering He has perfected forever those who are being sanctified."

"The sanctified" are all those who have trusted Christ, young and old, rich and poor, bond and free, male and female. We have all been placed by God "in Christ" and have been set apart for God (*sanctified*) forever. We may now approach a holy God directly, without a priest as an intermediary. That does not mean that we have become sinless. I am sure we are all painfully aware of our sinful natures, but as far as the books in Heaven are concerned, the account has been closed and the debt cancelled completely. We will never be called to answer for our sins. Yes, sin had to be judged, but the judgment fell on Christ and believers are set free.

All humanity now falls into two sections. One section is comprised of those who are sanctified and the other is made up of those who are not. There is no halfway position. It is impossible to be "almost saved". We are either saved (sanctified) or we are considered to be an enemy of God.

Verses 15-17:

"And the Holy Spirit also witnesses to us; for after He had said before, 16 "This is the covenant that I will make with them after those days, says the Lord: I will put My laws into their hearts, and in their minds I will write them," 17 then He adds, "Their sins and their lawless deeds I will remember no more."

Here, the writer quotes from Jeremiah 31:33. The prophet lived six centuries before the birth of Christ, yet already the plan of salvation was in progress. God could make that promise only because He knew that Jesus would one day come and pay the penalty for sin. The veil would remain in place until the transaction was settled. Many people today imagine that God forgives sin because He is merciful and loving but that is not so. He certainly is merciful and loving but He cannot overlook sin on those grounds. His perfection allows Him to forgive us only because the blood of His Son was shed as atonement. By that act, the barrier was removed and God is enabled to manifest His love on His creatures, even though they are still sinners by nature.

Verse 18:

"Now where there is remission of these, there is no longer an offering for sin."

Now that sin has been cancelled there is no longer any point in taking action to atone for it. That work has already been done. Human nature being what it is, some have great difficulty believing that they are free from condemnation. They are conscious of their sinful tendencies and feel that somehow they must pay for their wrong-doings. They imagine that God is still angry with them and that although they have given their hearts to the Lord Jesus, there still remains a distance between them and God. This is particularly common among those who committed serious sin in the past and who now live with guilt because of it. However, guilt is a burden which no Christian should carry. Regret, yes, but not guilt. Paul never forgot his vicious persecution of Christians before he was saved. He deeply regretted his actions. Yet he was able to write in Romans 8:1 *"There is therefore now no condemnation to those who are in Christ Jesus."* He was able to accept freedom from guilt because he believed that Jesus had settled the debt for him and wiped his account clean.

Guilt is sometimes perpetuated by faulty reasoning. People say, *"I know God has forgiven me but I cannot forgive myself."* That sounds heroic but in fact it displays the height of conceit. If almighty God has forgiven me, who am I to refuse to do so? Am I more righteous than God, more just than He? It is not enough to accept in my head that my account with God has been cleared. I must believe it in my heart and rejoice.

When our family first came to this country, I was given a loan by my employer. Each month I went to his office to make a payment. One day he asked me if I had the note with me and asked to see it. I handed it to him and he wrote across its face *"Paid in full."* Then he signed it and handed it back to me. I was a long way from actually paying off the loan but legally the debt had now disappeared. It no longer existed. I was free because of my employer's generosity and grace. It was a paradox. Most of the money that I had borrowed was still unpaid, yet the note said it was paid in full. God is also able to do that. Paul wrote in Romans 4:17 that God *"calls those things that are not as though they were."* You and I should not do that but God can because He is God.

Jesus made this all possible. If we persist in condemning ourselves, we actually question the sufficiency of Christ's atonement. We say, in effect, *"Yes, Jesus paid for all sin except mine!"* We must understand that the sacrifice of Christ paid for ALL sin, past, present and future, and accept the fact that God's justice was completely satisfied. Our account in Heaven is clean and our debt no longer exists. It was paid in full by Jesus Christ.

Verses 19-20:

"Therefore, brethren, having boldness to enter the Holiest by the blood of Jesus, 20 by a new and living way which He consecrated for us, through the veil, that is, His flesh,"

The word *"boldness"* in verse 19 means literally, *"all speech"* – a freedom to speak plainly and openly. This is possible only when the barriers have been removed between the parties. When guilt or fear exist, speech is inhibited. For the believer, guilt and fear have both been removed and we have the privilege of communicating freely with God directly. We have been given freedom to enter into the "holiest", where God dwells, and where nobody but the high priest dare ever go before Jesus came. We no longer need a human priest to intercede for us. We are told that Jesus Himself in our intermediary and *"ever lives to intercede for us."*

The way into God's presence is a new and living way, which Christ inaugurated for us. The way is *"through the veil"* which barred the people from God's presence for fourteen centuries. The wording of verse 20 makes it sound as if Christ's flesh was the veil but that is not the meaning. The flesh of Christ, broken on the cross, became the way through the veil. It is called a *"living way"* because Christ died and then rose again. It is by His *life* that we are saved. His living priesthood makes our access to the throne of God a reality. That is why we always approach God in the name of Jesus. In His company we can be confident, even in the throne-room of the universe!

Verses 21-22:

"and having a High Priest over the house of God, 22 let us draw near with a true heart in full assurance of faith, having our hearts sprinkled from an evil conscience and our bodies washed with pure water."

With Jesus as our representative we can have full assurance. The basis of this assurance is the cleansing which Jesus has achieved for us. The writer takes his analogies from the service in the tabernacle, and later, in the temple. The court contained two prominent articles - the brazen altar and the laver. The priest took the blood of the sacrifice and sprinkled it on the altar, and then he washed at the laver. Both actions spoke of cleansing. In type, our hearts are *"sprinkled"* from an evil conscience (referring to the altar) and we are *"washed with the pure water"* (referring to the laver). The important thing, as verse 22 specifies, is that we draw near *"with a true heart."* Our confidence can never be in ourselves. It must be in Him. We must believe with all our being that God is satisfied with what Jesus did and we approach Him, by faith, on those terms.

God says, *"Their sins and iniquities I will remember no more."* He does not say that He will *forget* our sins. He is not forgetful or absent minded. He is perfect, timeless and unencumbered by the weaknesses that plague the human race. God does not forget anything. He simply pledges that because our sins have been judicially paid for, He will remember them no longer. It is an act of His will. He will never bring them up, or even mention them again. A person who forgets something is likely to remember it again later. But this is a guarantee by God Himself that our sins are irrevocably put away.

There are people who accept the fact that all their sins were wiped from the record when they trusted Christ, but now they are worried by the sinful tendencies they see in their own lives every day. They feel that if they had truly been cleansed, these tendencies would no longer plague them. Consequently, they imagine that God is permanently angry with them. They find it difficult to believe that having given them a clean start when they were saved, He would go on forgiving them when they continued to fail over and over again. From a human standpoint that idea does make sense. But that is our problem. We see everything through human eyes and tend to transfer our own emotions to God. But God is not human; He is not limited to human logic. In Isaiah 55:8-9, God said,

> *"My thoughts are not your thoughts, neither are your ways my ways. For as the heavens are higher than the earth, so are my ways higher than your ways and my thoughts than your thoughts."*

Just as past sins were covered by the blood of Christ, so are present sins. Otherwise, there would be one settlement for sins that are past and another for sins that are present. Past sins were present sins yesterday and present sins will be past sins tomorrow. God doesn't live in time; He lives in eternity. To Him there is no past, present or future. Everything is alike to Him. That is how the writer to the Hebrews was able to write *"by one offering He has perfected for ever those who are sanctified."* God is omniscient – He knows everything. When He saved you, He knew everything you had done to that point and everything you would do from that point to the day you died, and He saved you just the same. He is never surprised when you fail. He knew before the world was made precisely when and how you would sin.

This truth, of course, does not give us a license to sin. We are exhorted to *"Walk worthy of the calling with which we are called."* But however hard we may try, we will fail many times because we are sinful by nature. God anticipates this. That is why, in 1 John 1:9 he says, *"If we confess our sins, He is faithful and just to forgive us our sins, and to cleanse us from all unrighteousness."* Notice the word *"all"* in that verse.

Holding fast our confession

Verse 23:

> *"Let us hold fast the confession of our hope without wavering, for He who promised is faithful."*

We owned a car once which developed an irritating problem. The battery kept going flat. No sooner did we recharge it but it went flat again. Eventually we discovered that the problem was not the battery at all but the alternator, whose function it was to keep the battery charged. The battery itself was OK but it was receiving insufficient nourishment to keep it doing its job. Now some Christians are like that. Their spiritual batteries keep going flat. They attend a conference or a seminar and they come home all charged up. They want to change the world. They set up morning devotions and evening devotions and family devotions and even volunteer to teach a Sunday school class. But just a few days later they are back in the doldrums. Somehow they have lost their charge. Prayer and Bible study are a drag again. Guilt plagues them because they feel they should be more excited about their faith. Sometimes they even begin to wonder if they are Christians at all! What we need is not a series of highs and lows but consistency and stability in our Christian lives and this is possible only as we learn to keep our spiritual batteries charged.

Now the writer to the Hebrews knew that. In this passage he puts his finger on the need. Some translators substitute the word "hope" for "faith", but faith is better. However, the words "confession" or "profession" require investigation. Both are closely related in the English language and they are both used to translate the same Greek word. They signify verbal declaration – something we say. If you are a Christian, your confession (or profession) is what you say about your faith. There is a well-known saying that goes: *"What you are speaks so loud that the world can't hear what you say."* In a sense that is true. People read our actions, attitudes and expressions, and formulate strong opinions based upon what they see. At election time this is particularly important. Words are cheap. Society is tired of hearing promises that are never fulfilled and voters tend to look at the record of the candidates before giving them their vote (they should do anyway). People want to know who you are before they listen to what you say.

However, the saying quoted above is only partly true. What we say is also important. You can't know what a Christian believes simply by watching him. He has to put it into words. Even God Himself chose words as His means of communication. Romans 10:9-10 make the case very clear:

> *"If you will confess with your mouth the Lord Jesus, and will believe in your heart that God has raised Him from the dead, you will be*

saved. 10 For with the heart man believes unto righteousness; and with the mouth confession is made unto salvation."

Actually, though those verses clarify the value of confession, they also raise questions which bother some believers. Elsewhere in the Scriptures we are told quite clearly that all a person needs to do to be saved is to believe. Verbal confession is not mentioned. When the Philippian jailor asked what he must do to be saved, Paul and Silas told him simply, *"Believe on the Lord Jesus Christ and you will be saved."* The solution seems fairly clear. Just as you cannot have true fire without heat, so you cannot have true faith without confession. One is the natural outflow from the other. If you have discovered something life-changing it is not natural to keep it quiet. On the Day of Pentecost, when the Holy Spirit entered into the disciples, they were so filled with excitement that they left the room where they had been hiding from the Jewish authorities, spilled out into the streets of Jerusalem and boldly shared their new-found faith. They were irrepressible; they could not be silenced. Their belief was vocalized, not by rules of law but by the sheer joy of life that welled up within them.

Confession does not necessarily involve standing on a street corner shouting the message to those who pass by. Very few believers could do that naturally and very few people are attracted by that approach. What it does involve is (in the words of Peter) *"Being ready to give an answer to anyone who asks you a reason for the hope that is in you."* Giving an answer before the question is asked often has a negative result. Many well-meaning Christians turn people away by being too aggressive with their witness. However, when someone observes the difference in a Christian's life style and asks for an explanation, the way is open for a powerful witness to be given. On such an occasion we should know clearly what we believe and why we believe it and be ready to speak up boldly.

Mutual consideration

Verse 24:

"And let us consider one another in order to stir up love and good works "

The word *"consider"* means *"to perceive clearly, to look closely."* Most of us tend to be somewhat superficial in our relationships. We "see" one another without really seeing. After the service in the average church there is a babble of conversation. People talk to people all over the sanctuary but most of the conversations take place between groups of friends. Visitors may leave feeling lonely and unwanted because nobody notices them, or seeks to draw them in. In this verse we are told to "consider" one another. People need to be noticed for what they are. Kind actions are provocative. They bring a response from the hearts of the individuals receiving them. We are specifically exhorted to "provoke" people in this way, not to anger but to love. True love produces love and by showing love to those around us (friends and strangers alike) we stir up within them a similar response. Instead of feeling rejected or ignored they go away with warm feeling of acceptance.

Verse 25:

"Not forsaking the assembling of ourselves together, as is the manner of some, but exhorting one another, and so much the more as you see the Day approaching."

When we forsake the assembling of ourselves together we simply stop going to church. Invariably something is wrong inside when this happens (unless the reason is sickness or incapacity). Maybe we have grown cold in our faith, or we don't like the pastor. Maybe someone has said or done something to offend us or we like hymns and the worship director insists on singing praise songs. Maybe we've written numerous notes to him, complaining about the music, but he doesn't change. And those drums!

Complaints such as these all suggest that our motive for attending church in the first place was to receive personal satisfaction rather than to worship. When our cherished opinion is thwarted our response is to quit. We "pick up our marbles and go home." That attitude is certainly not in sympathy with the Holy Spirit because in this verse He specifically forbids it. The root cause can usually be traced to self-centeredness. *My* personal taste has been violated, or *I* have been offended, or *I* don't agree with some decision the church board has made. But we shouldn't attend church for what we can get out of it. We should go to worship the Lord and to serve others. If we are concerned only with ourselves, we fail to grasp the purpose of assembling together with fellow believers. There is a verse in John's first letter that is very challenging. It says: *"By this we know that we have passed from death unto life; because we love the brethren."* Apart from worshipping the Lord, our love for the brethren should prompt us to attend church. If we lack that love, we would be wise to question our salvation.

The last phrase of verse 25 makes another serious observation. It is becoming increasingly important to be in a good relationship with the Lord and with the Christian family because time is running short. *"The Day is approaching."* Every time the sun sets we are one day nearer to the Lord's return. Nobody knows when He will come but He has promised to do so at a time when we least expect Him. Satan knows this and is intensifying his activities. If ever there was a need for mutual love and encouragement it is now. How sad it would be for the Lord to return and find us boycotting the services due to some personal grudge, or a backslidden state! As Paul wrote to the Romans, *". . . knowing the time, that now it is high time to awake out of sleep; for now is our salvation nearer than when we believed."* Romans 13:11.

No other sacrifice

Verses 26-27:

"For if we sin willfully after we have received the knowledge of the truth, there no longer remains a sacrifice for sins, 27 but a certain fearful expectation of judgment, and fiery indignation which will devour the adversaries."

We all sin, Christians and non-Christians alike. Furthermore, we sin willfully. We like to think of our sins as mistakes, or that the devil made us do it, or that somebody else was responsible. This tendency is as old as Genesis 3, where Adam blamed Eve and Eve blamed the serpent for their sin. The truth is that all sin is willful. We have no excuse. What, then, do verses 26 and 27 tell us? Do they condemn us all to judgment? At first glance they may seem to, but in fact they do not.

The sense of verses 26-27 is logical enough. God has provided just one remedy for sin. That remedy is Jesus Christ. There is no other. Jesus said, *"No man comes to the Father except by me."* Consequently, if we reject the only remedy God has given to us we are without hope. We shut ourselves off from God and condemn ourselves to judgment. Verse 26 warns that if an individual is presented with the way of salvation and willfully rejects it, there is no alternative sacrifice for him to claim. Christians need have no fear of these verses. Believers have already availed themselves of God's solution. Judgment, for them, is past because Jesus took their place and suffered the judgment on their behalf.

The judgment will surely come, of course, and those who have rejected Christ will have to face it. Verse 27 is terrifying in the picture it paints. Words like *"certain"*, *"fearful"*, *"fiery"* and *"devouring"* describe a cataclysmic event beyond human imagination. But it can be avoided by simply turning to the Lord Jesus and trusting Him for refuge. 1 John 4:17-18 refers to this truth. It says:

> *"Herein is our love made perfect, that we may have boldness in the Day of Judgment: because as He is, so are we in this world. 18 There is no fear in love; but perfect love casts out fear: because fear has torment, He who fears is not made perfect in love."*

The fear in these verses has to do with judgment. People fear the judgment but Christians have no reason to fear. God, who is perfect love, casts out the fear of judgment and gives them the assurance that *"as He is, so are they in this world."* In other words, believers have been given a garment of righteousness, which covers their sin and makes them acceptable in God's sight. God looks at the Christian and sees Jesus. We have been made "like Him."

The next four verses continue to speak of the inevitable consequence of rejecting the offer of salvation through Jesus Christ and of its Old Testament equivalent.

The foolishness of unbelief

Verses 28-31:

> *"Anyone who has rejected Moses' law dies without mercy on the testimony of two or three witnesses. 29 Of how much worse punishment, do you suppose, will he be thought worthy who has trampled the Son of God underfoot, counted the blood of the*

covenant by which he was sanctified a common thing, and insulted the Spirit of grace? 30 For we know Him who said, "Vengeance is Mine; I will repay, says the Lord." And again, "The Lord will judge His people." 31 It is a fearful thing to fall into the hands of the living God."

Deuteronomy 17:2-7 makes it clear that any man or woman convicted of worshipping the sun, moon or any other gods was to be brought before the congregation and executed by stoning. No loop holes or plea agreements were allowed but it was stipulated that there had to be two witnesses to the offense. One accuser was not sufficient to secure judgment. Here the writer is challenging the reader to answer his question. "If the people of Israel were subjected to such a severe law, how much more would someone deserve punishment if he "*has trampled the Son of God underfoot, counted the blood of the covenant by which he was sanctified a common thing, and insulted the Spirit of grace?*" By ignoring, or rejecting, God's offer of salvation, a person tramples the name of Christ underfoot and insults the Holy Spirit.

Notice the words "*wherewith he was sanctified*" towards the end of verse 29. Some point to this verse and claim that since only true Christians are sanctified, this must be evidence that a believer could fall from grace and lose his salvation. However, in the light of the cross, *everybody* is potentially sanctified. Christ's death atoned for the sins of the whole world (1 John 2:2). He died to cancel all sin –period-- not only the sins of Christians. His is not an ongoing sacrifice. He does not die afresh when we believe; He died over two thousand years ago, and we are asked to place our faith in what Jesus did in AD 33. The work has been done for two thousand years. When we believe, we enter into an established position. We could walk up to any man or woman in the street and tell them that Christ died for them and that their sins are already paid for. That is the good news. They may not believe what we say but that doesn't alter the truth. Our belief, or lack of it, does not change history. It is when the Spirit of Grace reveals our need to us that we believe it and are saved. If we were to refuse, we would insult the Spirit's testimony.

The need for endurance

Verses 32-34:

"But recall the former days in which, after you were illuminated, you endured a great struggle with sufferings: 33 partly while you were made a spectacle both by reproaches and tribulations, and partly while you became companions of those who were so treated. 34 for you had compassion on me in my chains, and joyfully accepted the plundering of your goods, knowing that you have a better and an enduring possession for yourselves in heaven."

As in any period, there was a divergence of position among the original recipients of this letter. Most of them were genuine believers but a few were "almost persuaded" and in danger of slipping back into the old ways. Others were weak in their faith and were beginning to wonder if their new faith was worth the price they were asked to pay for it. In all probability, these people lived in Rome, where conditions were destined to get worse. The writer therefore covered his bases. He reminded them of their past record, how they had held up valiantly under all kinds of adversity. Apparently, most of them had not yet suffered the extremes of persecution, such as that experienced by the Palestinian Christians, involving imprisonment and death, but they had been publicly humiliated and their property had been confiscated because they had boldly identified with the few who had been arrested. What they needed was encouragement and this letter was designed to meet that need.

Verses 35-37:

"Therefore do not cast away your confidence, which has great reward. 36 For you have need of endurance, so that after you have done the will of God, you may receive the promise: 37 "For yet a little while, And He who is coming will come and will not tarry."

"Confidence" amounts to faith, doesn't it? If we place our confidence in ourselves, which many do, we are sure to fail, no matter how strong or resourceful we may imagine ourselves to be, but if we place our confidence in Christ, He will see us through. *"Endurance"* is the ability

to keep on keeping on in the face of all odds, keeping our eyes on the promise of the Lord's return.

The promise of Christ's coming

Some ridicule this concept. They point out that Paul expected the Lord to return in his lifetime, which came to an end two thousand years ago. Since then, countless generations have lived out their lives with the same expectation, only to die unfulfilled. However, Jesus never stated the time of His return. He promised that it would happen when we least expect it and that no man could predict when it would take place. In fact, He specifically taught that even the heavenly host did not know the time or date of the great event. In his second letter, Peter wrote about this very thing. He wrote:

> *"Knowing this first, that there will come in the last days scoffers, walking after their own lusts, 4 saying, where is the promise of His coming? For since the fathers fell asleep, all things continue as they were from the beginning of creation."*

Peter knew, back then, that people would laugh at the idea of Christ coming back to earth. But in the following verses he warns that such a position is based upon an arrogant ignorance of God's Word, that the same God who created the earth and caused the Great Flood to cover the earth because of man's wickedness would one day destroy the earth with fire. Then, in verses 8-9 of the same chapter, he continues:

> *"But beloved, be not ignorant of this one thing, that one day is with the Lord as a thousand years, and a thousand years as one day. The Lord is not slack concerning His promise, as some men count slackness, but is longsuffering toward us, not willing that any should perish, but that all should come to repentance."* (2 Peter 3:3-4, 8-9)

One day Christ will return as a thief in the night and even though millennia have passed since He made His promise, it is still valid, and we should be actively expecting Him to come at any time. Previous generations have been "kept on their toes" by the expectation of the Lord's arrival and we should follow their example.

The just shall live by faith

Verse 38-39:

"Now the just shall live by faith; but if anyone draws back, my soul has no pleasure in him." 39 But we are not of those who draw back to perdition, but of those who believe to the saving of the soul."

Here is the key to verses 28-31. There are two clear groups of people: those who draw back to perdition and those who believe to the saving of the soul. Those who draw back are obviously not Christians. Those who go on obviously are. This is a parallel passage to the difficult section back in chapter 6, where, after warning of the impossibility of finding an alternative route to salvation after rejecting Christ, he says: *"But beloved, we are persuaded better things of you, and things that accompany salvation, though we thus speak."* Clearly, he makes a demarcation between the saved and the unsaved.

Verse 38 is a quotation from Habakkuk 2:4. Which, (quoted again in Romans 1:17) played such an important part in the Reformation. It struck at the foundation of error which had been taught for so long. Faith, not self-effort, is the key to salvation. The result of failing to trust in the living God will be to draw back when the going gets rough.

When I was a young boy, about 11 or 12, I went to school each morning on the train. There were seven or eight other kids who travelled with me and among them was a girl named Rosie. Rosie was a couple of years older than I, taller, and had red cheeks. In her school uniform she looked quite matronly. However, she had a mother's heart and she used to call me "Little One", which did nothing to boost my ego. Well, in order to reach the station I had to cycle about three miles and sometimes, when the wind blew against me, I would be late for the train.

On one particular occasion I was behind time and after depositing my bike in the shed where we left them, and running with all my might through the tunnel under the station, I leapt up the stone steps to the platform just as the train was beginning to move out. Well, Rosie saw me, opened the door and shouted with a loud voice, "Come on Little One, you can make it!" I looked at the train as it gathered speed and was not sure I shared her confidence. A porter nearby saw the situation, grabbed me round the waist and ran along beside the train with me, while all the other kids poked their heads out of windows as Rosie screamed, "Come on Little One! Come on Little One! You can make it!" But I was scared. The train was so big and was moving fast, so I drew back. Soon the porter gave up and put me down.

But I can still see the train as it faded into the distance, leaving me alone on the deserted station. And I fancy I can still hear Rosie's shrill voice, as she leaned far out of the window, waving her handkerchief and shouting, "Good bye Little One! Good bye Little One! Good bye Little One!" until she eventually disappeared in a cloud of steam.

My failure to take hold of the opportunity resulted only in my being late for school. I merely had to wait for the next train. But failure to take hold of the salvation that is being held out to us will result in the Lake of Fire. There will be no "next train" when that time comes; only a fearful expectation of judgment. We must not draw back; we must reach forward and grasp the hand that is being held out to help.

CHAPTER 11

This chapter is popularly known as *"The Faith Chapter"* because it covers two important aspects of the believer's experience. The first is the definition of faith (what faith *is*). The second is the demonstration of faith (what faith *does*). Both of these aspects must be grasped by the Christian if he is to function adequately in his daily walk.

The definition of faith

Faith is of immense importance to the Christian. Take it away and there is nothing left. The Bible tells us that we are *saved* by faith (Ephesians 2:8), that we are *justified* by faith (Romans 3:28), that we have *access to God* by faith (Romans 5:2), that we are to *live* by faith (Romans 1:17) and that without faith it is impossible to please God (Hebrews 11:6). Romans 14:23 even goes so far as to say that *"Whatsoever is not of faith is sin!"* It doesn't take much imagination to grasp the seriousness of this truth.

However, the question is not so much whether faith is important (I think we would all agree that it is), but whether or not we understand it. Do we grasp its function? Is it possible that due to an imperfect idea of what faith really is, our Christian walk could be jeopardized? I believe this is entirely possible. James, in his letter, touches on this subject. He claims that faith which does not result in action is dead. To better understand his argument, I'd like to analyze the passage before we move on. In James 2:14 he writes:

> *"What does it profit, my brethren, though a man say he has faith and has not works. Can faith save him?"*

The answer, of course, is "Yes. It can save him." The authority for this assertion is Romans 3:28, which says that *"a man is justified by faith, without the works of the law.*" However, James is not claiming that true faith does not save. He is questioning the validity of what some of us accept as faith. True faith is not passive; it is active and should so change our lives that it influences everything we do and say.

The next two verses give a simple illustration of a belief system that is not carried through into action.

> "*If a brother or sister be naked and destitute of daily food, and one say to them, Depart in peace, be warmed and filled: notwithstanding you give them not those things that are needful to the body; what does it profit?*"

Obviously that is not a picture of faith; it is not intended to be. It illustrates inconsistency. The words, "*depart in peace, be warmed and filled*" indicate intellectual concern, while failure to act demonstrates that the heart is not touched. Genuine compassion for the needy person is missing. James is speaking in general terms and offers the illustration simply as a "for instance." Some have misinterpreted the passage and assumed that in order to display faith they must care for the bodily needs of hungry people. Such activity is admirable but not necessarily proof of faith. Many people who make no profession of faith at all help to relieve suffering in the world. Their works certainly show compassion but they don't demonstrate faith because they have no faith to display. James is referring to any actions that demonstrate faith, not necessarily mercy.

Then James continues:

> "*Even so, faith without works is dead, being alone.*"

Just as the concern was dead in the previous passage, so faith is dead when it does not result in a practical outworking in our lives.

James then writes,

> "*Yes, a man may say, you have faith and I have works: Show me your faith without works and I will show you my faith by my works. You believe that there is one God. You do well. The demons also believe and tremble.*"

James is now moving near to his point. It is common for people to claim that because they believe in God, they must be Christians. In fact, they are no nearer salvation than are the demons because the demons believe that much and tremble before Him. There is a huge difference between a person who simply believes that God exists and another who surrenders to God's claims. A person may believe that God exists, that He is the creator of all things, reigns upon the throne of the universe and sent Jesus to die on the cross for our sins, but still not be saved.

Finally in the James 2 passage, verses 20-21:

"Will you know, O vain man, that faith without works is dead? Was not Abraham justified by works when he offered up Isaac, his son, upon the altar? Can you see how faith wrought with his works, and by works, faith was made perfect? And the Scripture was fulfilled, which says: Abraham believed God and it was credited to him for righteousness."

Abraham did not demonstrate his faith by feeding and clothing hungry people, or by doing any of the things which people think of as "works" today. Such actions would have demonstrated compassion, but Abraham's "works" indicated a deeper level of faith than that. By being willing to offer up his son, he demonstrated that he was willing to obey God, even though God's request seemed unreasonable, and cut across everything Abraham had lived for all those years! That is the principle which needs to be carried over into your life and mine.

The "works" of faith have deeper roots than kindness and goodness. They are planted in unquestioning obedience to the will of God. The will of God is laid out for us in the Word of God, and as we shall see, true faith always results in practical obedience to God's Word, even if that obedience means denying one's own desires and ambitions.

There is a lot of "faith" today that does not produce obedience. It is therefore of great importance that as we study the "Faith Chapter" we think hard about our own faith. Does it pass the test?

Is it the kind of faith that is described here in Hebrews 11 or does it fall into the merely intellectual category that James describes in his letter?

Chapter 11

Faith defined

Hebrews 11, verse 1:

"Now faith is the substance of things hoped for, the evidence of things not seen."

The longer one meditates on this verse, the deeper it becomes. Since faith itself is intangible it is difficult to define succinctly. This verse makes a masterful attempt. Christians rely heavily on a number of unusual things. These fall into one of two main categories: "Things hoped for" and "Things not seen." Unseen things play a large part in our faith. The *existence and sovereignty of God Himself* are unseen. (*"No man has seen God at any time."*) In the Bible we learn that He rules the universe, and we see evidence to support the Bible's claim but we cannot prove it scientifically. *Forgiveness of sin* is another unseen factor in the Christian faith. How do we know that it exists? Certainly we cannot see or touch forgiveness. Yet we need it and rely upon it as a basic requirement of our belief system. *The end of sin and its consequences* is another example of things unseen. The Bible states clearly that sin was dealt with, once for all, at the cross but there is no way we could check that out with our senses. We are two thousand years too late to do that, and half a world away from the location where it took place. Even had we lived at the time of Christ, and seen the Lord die, we could not have proved that sin had been finally overcome.

Everlasting life is also unseen. Jesus said that anyone believing in Him will not perish but will have everlasting life. Where would we be without that? Yet we cannot prove it. We cannot see it. We are simply asked to believe because God's Word promises it. How about *the second coming of Christ*? That also is unseen and impossible to prove. 1 Corinthians 15 contains a whole section about the nature and characteristics of the new bodies we shall receive, but nobody has seen one. We are asked to accept the promise contained only in the Word of God. Even *Heaven itself* is unseen. John saw it in a vision and wrote down a little of what he saw, but we can't share John's privilege. Nobody even knows even where heaven is and none of our departed friends or relatives have ever returned to tell us about it. None of these things is seen but faith grasps them because they comprise the very heart of Christianity. Faith is the evidence of things not seen.

"Things hoped for" produce a similar problem. They are inaudible and intangible. They have not yet taken place and we can only vaguely imagine what they will be like. Yet faith enables us to hold on to them as if they had already taken place because God promised them and we rest in Him. We rely totally upon Him to fulfill them. At the rapture, we shall not be able to propel ourselves into the sky to meet the Lord. Unless He takes us up, we shall remain exactly where we are. Nor could we create the new body He promises us. That metamorphosis is entirely in His hands. Our entrance into Heaven is another subject for hope, yet utterly unattainable in our own strength. Our confidence must be in the promises of God.

Faith changes the meaning of "*hope*" from a wish to a blessed certainty. It is the *evidence* of things unseen and the *substance* of things hoped for. Without faith in the promises of God, believers would have no security, no assurance. But when we truly believe that He is incapable of lying and that His promises are absolute certainties, we are given a confidence which cannot be shaken by life's ups and downs. By faith, God's promises take on a substance of their own. We still cannot see them but they become almost tangible. We can rely upon them and base our hope upon them with complete assurance. One day this world will pass away. As we saw in chapter one, the Lord will fold up the heavens like a garment. But God's promises remain unchanged. They are eternal. They are unaffected by the most cataclysmic event imaginable and they are irrevocable.

One Saturday morning in the spring of 1980, a package arrived at our home in England. It contained a letter from Dr. John Hunter, together with a number of other papers. In his letter, Dr. Hunter wrote"

> "*My dear friends, this package is going to come as a surprise to you! I am wondering if and how the Lord is preparing your hearts to read its contents. The contents are self-explanatory in a way. Sufficient to say that these people are well-known to me. . .. . I feel you are just the man for the job, but the Lord is the one to decide. God bless you*

*as you plunge into this situation. It is April 1ˢᵗ – an opportunity to
be a fool for Christ! Much love, John."*

As you might have guessed, the package contained a letter from a church
in Idaho, inviting me to consider the possibility of becoming its pastor.
It certainly was an exciting morning. We were taken completely by
surprise. The point I want to make is that by the end of that month we
were invited to leave our home in England and fly 6,000 miles to a place
we had never heard of, in order to minister to a congregation we had
never seen. To some, that might seem to be an unreasonable request and
for us to accept such an offer might appear irresponsible, but what made
the difference was the letter from John Hunter. We knew the author and
we trusted him. To us, his character was *"the evidence of things unseen."*
Of course, in the last analysis we trusted the Lord, but the principle still
holds true. In October of that year, my family and I boarded a plane in
London and took off into the sky, completely blind as to the future. But
we knew John had been there before us and we trusted him.

As Christians, that is how everything we do should be. As far as our
sight is concerned, the future is a blank screen. But when we know and
trust the Author of the Word upon which we stand, we can set out with
confidence, resting in the knowledge that He has already been where
He has asked us to go, and He would not send us there unless He knew
that going there was in our best interests. Paul wrote: *"For the things
that are seen are temporal, but the things that are not seen are eternal."*
It is the Person of Christ Himself in whom we must place our trust.
Some translations change the word *"substance"* to *"assurance."* *"Blessed
assurance, Jesus is mine."* (That is the present tense --*"things unseen."*)
"O, what a foretaste of glory divine." (That is the future tense – *"Things
hoped for."*)

Verse 2:

"For by it the elders obtained a good testimony."

In this verse the people referred to collectively as "elders" obtained a
good report by putting their faith to work. They believed what God said
and acted accordingly, even though, in some cases, it cost them their
lives. Vincent writes: *"Faith apprehends as a real fact what is not revealed*

to the senses. It rests upon that fact, acts upon it, and is upheld by it in the face of all that seems to contradict it. Faith is real seeing." (Word Studies in the New Testament, Volume 4, page 509).

The Demonstration of faith

The next verse introduces the second section of this chapter, which has to do with how faith behaves under testing. Faith does not exist in isolation. We cannot store up faith as we might store water in a reservoir. It has no shelf-life at all. Faith is an attitude, a philosophy if you like, which exists only when we use it in life's situations. Just as the engine of a car achieves nothing until it begins to turn the wheels, so faith is meaningless until it begins to dictate our reaction to life's challenges. This chapter demonstrates from the lives of well-known Old Testament characters exactly how faith operates. As we examine each one, we could ask ourselves the question, **"What does faith *say* when put to the test?** Obviously it doesn't "say" anything audibly but the heart's attitude under stress can be expressed in words. In each case, the question can be answered beginning with the words, "I will," which speaks of volition. True faith demonstrates itself by a willingness to do God's will – a decision to be obedient.

Verse 3:

"By faith we understand that the worlds were framed by the word of God, so that the things which are seen were not made of things which are visible."

1.   Faith says, ***"I will accept the Bible as the truth."***

The truth of Scripture is flatly denied by much of society today. In this country, the schools and universities refuse to accept God's creation as truth. In its place, they teach our young people atheistic theory which denies and contradicts the Genesis record. The authority of God's Word is rejected and replaced with human theory.

God's creation of the universe is found only in the Bible. The teaching can be supported in various outside ways but it cannot be proved. It must be accepted by faith. By rejecting creation, we reject the Scriptures also, and we are on our own. The scientific substitutes being taught to our young people cannot be proved either. They also must be accepted by faith. The theory of evolution raises more questions than answers but it is more palatable to the unregenerate mind than the teaching of creation because it bypasses God. If creation were accepted, God would have to be acknowledged, and if God were acknowledged His sovereignty would also have to be accepted. Under those circumstances, man would be forced to accept responsibility for his sin and recognize his need of salvation. That would be too much to ask of our liberal educators.

The base and beginning of the subject of faith is trust in the reliability of the Bible. If we reject any part of it we reject it all. By placing our intellect above the Scriptures, we set ourselves up as judges of revealed truth. This verse speaks of origin. The scriptures tell us that God spoke the universe into being from nothing and faith says, "*I will accept the Bible as truth.*"

2. Faith says**, "*I will approach God on God's terms.*"**

Verse 4:

"*By faith Abel offered to God a more excellent sacrifice than Cain, through which he obtained witness that he was righteous, God testifying of his gifts; and through it he being dead still speaks.*"

Cain and Abel were the first two people ever to be naturally born into this world. Both of their parents had been created miraculously by God. In Genesis 3 we read their story. Cain was a tiller of the ground and Abel was a keeper of sheep. Both men believed in God but they had different ideas about approaching Him. Cain brought the fruit of the ground as an offering but Abel brought the firstlings of his flock. We are told that God accepted Abel's offering but rejected Cain's.

These brothers were equal before God. Both had been born outside Eden, after Adam's fall, and both had inherited their father's fallen nature. Consequently, both were sinners, estranged from God and in need of His mercy. Both had to approach God by means of an offering but each chose a different route.

I am sure there was nothing wrong with the produce Cain brought.

It was no doubt the best available, probably washed and scrubbed like you see at the county fair. But we cannot approach God on the basis of beauty, effort or achievement. God is unimpressed by these things. By contrast, Abel acted in faith. The Bible says that *"Faith comes by hearing and hearing by the Word of God."* Both brothers must have heard their father recount his story – how God had clothed him and Eve with coats of skins after they sinned. Something had to die before the skins were available. No doubt Adam explained how his own efforts at covering their sin were unacceptable to God and how they could approach Him only on the basis of a lamb's blood. The Bible doesn't tell us these details but it is inconceivable that Adam failed to instruct his sons concerning such important matters.

Cain and Abel both heard the way explained but Cain chose to ignore it and substituted his own way. Predictably it failed. *"There is a way that seems right to man, but its end is the way of death."* (Proverbs 4:12). By contrast, Abel heard and obeyed. He approached God trusting in the shed blood of the lamb, not necessarily because he understood but because God demanded it. He exercised faith. He said, in effect, "This is the way God said I must approach Him and so I will follow His instructions, even though I do not fully understand." The lamb stood for Jesus, who would one day come to save mankind. Nothing has changed through the millennia. There is still no channel by which we may approach God, other than via the Lord Jesus, *"the Lamb slain before the foundation of the world."*

We read that *"by it (his sacrifice) he (Abel) obtained witness that he was righteous."* This did not mean that he was righteous in himself. He was a sinner, like every other human being. Nor was he demonstrated to be righteous by bringing the correct sacrifice. He was *decreed* righteous because he trusted in the blood of the lamb. The death of the lamb, picturing the death of Christ, thousands of years later, was credited to him, and his faith was accounted to him for righteousness.

As we shall see in verse 28, on the night of the Passover, the children of Israel were no more righteous than the Egyptians who followed them. They were all sinners. The only difference was that the Israelites hid themselves behind the blood of the lamb and the Egyptians did not. God told them, *"When I see the blood I will pass over you."* Had the

Israelites elected to protect themselves some other way, they would have suffered the same fate as the Egyptians. It was the blood that made the difference, plus their faith in it, not the fact that they were Israelites.

The final clause of verse 4 says: *"and through it he being dead still speaks."* What does he say? It can be only one thing, namely, *"This is the way, walk ye in it."* From his place in ancient antiquity Abel holds up the light and says to you and to me, *"Follow my example. Place your faith in the blood of the lamb. It is the only way God recognizes."* In a way, Cain still speaks also, but he is disseminating a warning to those who, like him, choose to go their own way instead of following God's instructions.

3.   Faith says, ***"I will please God by trusting Him."***

Verses 5-6:

"By faith Enoch was translated so that he did not see death, and was not found because God had translated him; for before his translation he had this testimony, that he pleased God

We don't know very much about Enoch. In Genesis 5:21-24 we read a brief outline of his life. We read that he lived a total 365 years and was the father of Methuselah; we also learn that he walked with God and did not see death because he was translated at the end of his life. In verse 5 we are told that Enoch *"pleased God"* and in verse 6 we learn that the only way to please God is by exercising faith. Enoch therefore pleased God by trusting Him. The overwhelming agreement among Bible students is that he was "raptured" (taken up alive to meet God in Heaven). Some question this interpretation and claim that Heaven is not mentioned. This is true, but it would be difficult to avoid the clear statements regarding Enoch's departure from this earth. He walked with God; he did not see death; suddenly he was not present because God took him.

Verse 6:

"But without faith it is impossible to please Him, for he who comes to God must believe that He is, and that He is a rewarder of those who diligently seek Him."

Very few people who believe in God's existence would not wish to please Him. The problem is that a great number of them would be unable to correctly answer the question: *"What must we do to please God?"* A variety of solutions might be offered. Some might say, *"Be good; live a good life."* Others might say *"Don't swear, don't smoke, don't lie, cheat or steal."* Still others might say, *"Live by the Ten Commandments, or the Golden Rule."* In every case they would be wrong. There is only one way to please God and that is by trusting Him.

Verse 6 makes that crystal clear. *"Without faith it is impossible to please Him."* Notice, the writer does not say it would be *difficult* to please Him. It says it is *impossible*. Thus faith becomes the unavoidable requisite. But what does faith entail? According to this verse, it demands two parallel convictions: a) believing that God "is", and b) believing that He is a rewarder of those who diligently seek Him. On the face of it, those two conditions may seem rather simplistic. Someone reading the verse casually might think, *"Well, that's easy enough. I can do that. I already believe there is a God and I guess I kind of believe He rewards those who seek Him."* But to think this way would be to miss the whole meaning of the passage.

First, we please God by believing that He "is". Is what? Is God! That is not as silly as it sounds. Believing that God exists without recognizing His absolute sovereignty over all things, including our own lives, would be a contradiction in terms. A God who is not in total control is fictitious. If God "is", then He has the right to dictate whatever terms He pleases, without being questioned, ignored or neglected in any way. If God "is", then He is the absolute designer, creator, ruler and controller of history, before whom we must bow and to whom we must surrender!

The second conviction softens and warms that awareness of God's person, without reducing it in any way. Not only is He absolute power, but He is also absolute *love*. He is the rewarder of those who diligently seek Him. When we recognize God to be God and desire to do His will, He is quick to respond. Not only does He forgive our sin and take us into His family, but He rewards us by allowing us to know Him.

Jesus said, *"This is life eternal, that they might know Thee, the only true God, and Jesus Christ whom Thou hast sent."* Our task is to walk each day by faith, as Enoch did, recognizing God for whom and what He is, and seeking to obey Him. If we do that, then (from the way things look right now) we might easily be translated as Enoch was, bodily into the Lord's presence without dying! In any case, we are guaranteed an eternity in His presence.

4. Faith says: "*I will heed God's warnings.*"

Verse 7:

"By faith Noah, being divinely warned of things not yet seen, moved with fear, prepared an ark for the saving of his household, by which he condemned the world and became heir of the righteousness which is according to faith."

Question: Why did Noah build the ark? Answer: Because he was moved by fear. Question: Why was he moved by fear? Answer: Because God had issued a warning about things to come and Noah believed that He meant what He said. That is a basic requirement of faith. Was Noah afraid of God? Yes, he was afraid, in the sense that he believed God would carry out His plan. A careful reading of Genesis 6:5-22 makes this crystal clear. God warned Noah out of love. He was not obligated to warn anyone but love motivated God's warning. He warned Noah well in advance – 120 years in advance to be exact! During that time Noah shared God's warning with the people of his day. 2 Peter 2:5 describes him as "*a preacher of righteousness.*" And 1 Peter 3:20 tells us that God waited patiently while the ark was being built. God issued the warning and then waited for 120 years, during which time Noah built the ark and preached righteousness to the people upon whom the judgment had been decreed.

Noah never doubted that God meant what He had said, and throughout those years, he walked with God by faith. What was the result? He and his family were saved. Did the ark save them? No! Faith saved them. The ark was merely the demonstration of Noah's faith. I feel sure that those 120 years were not the easiest of Noah's life. It is obvious from the Biblical account that none of the people to whom he preached believed what he told them. If any had believed, they would have surely shared the ark with Noah and his family. As a preacher, Noah must have felt a failure. However, he was a *faithful* failure! God does not measure our success by how many converts we make, or how popular we are. He measures it by how faithful we are to His Word.

We must remember that God did not cease to issue warnings after the flood. They continued, and just as God carried out His warnings in Noah's day, so He will surely carry out the warnings He has given to us. For instance, He has said in His Word: "*Be not deceived, God is not mocked: for whatsoever a man sows, that shall he also reap. He who sows to his flesh, shall of the flesh reap corruption; but he who sows to the Spirit, shall of the Spirit reap life everlasting.*"

That is a warning plus a promise and God means what He says. His Word also says, "*For it is appointed unto man once to die, and after that, the judgment.*" In Revelation 20:15, we read that "*whoever was not found written in the book of life was cast into the Lake of Fire.*" Yet an increasing number of people choose to discount these warnings. The fear of God is in short supply. As in the days of Noah, it is no longer politically correct to mention God's name (except in profanity) and even some of those who profess to know Christ live as if the warnings of God did not exist, or as if God didn't mean what He said. They sow to the flesh, and when they reap a bitter harvest; they blame God for being unfair, as if they had a special privilege that exempted them from the truth of Scripture.

Just as a son loves his father, but fears the chastening his father will give him if he steps out of line, so we should have the same fear of God. It is not a fear based on uncertainty or foreboding, as if God were in some way unreasonable or cruel, but one based on the security which clearly defined boundaries produce. In effect God says, "*Step over this line and this will happen.*" Faith believes what God says, and because we don't want "this" to happen, we keep within the limits God has set. God told Eve, "If you eat of this fruit you will die." She could heed the warning or leave it. She and her husband chose to disregard it and, sure enough, they died spiritually. By contrast, Noah believed God's warning and as the result, he and his entire household were saved from the judgment when it came.

5. Faith says, "*I will forsake the old way.*"

Verse 8:

"By faith Abraham obeyed when he was called to go out to the place which he would afterward receive as an inheritance. And he went out, not knowing where he was going."

Once again, faith resulted in obedience. God says it, faith believes it and belief results in action. The original passage in Genesis 12 records the beginning of Abram's story.

"Now the Lord had said to Abram, Get out from your country, and from your kindred, and from your father's house, unto a land that I will show you: And I will make you a great nation, and I will bless you and make your name great; and you shall be a blessing. And I will bless those who bless you and curse those who curse you, and in you shall all the families of the earth be blessed. So Abram departed, as the Lord had spoken to him, and Lot went with him. And Abram was seventy five years old when he departed out of Haran."

In response to God's instructions, he left his home in Haran and travelled west, trusting the Lord to guide him to a destination which God would later reveal. Here, the writer to the Hebrews tells us that Abram took this action by faith. His faith was demonstrated, not so much by going to another land as by leaving his own. He had a choice to make. He could remain in Ur, where things were familiar, comfortable and convenient (and heathen) or he could step out and claim God's promise. He could not do both.

God's terms were quite clear. Separation from the old life was the price he would have to pay for the blessing, but if he would obey, God would reward Abram by building his descendents into a great nation. In addition, God would support him by blessing those who blessed him and cursing those who cursed him, so that in Abraham all the families of the earth would be blessed.

There are degrees of belief. Abram might have believed what God promised intellectually but not sufficiently to do anything about it. He might have remained in Ur, and simply talked about the promise God had once made to him. But in departing from the land of his birth he demonstrated his faith to be real. Ur, where he lived, was a prosperous city. He lived in a highly developed society. There were libraries containing works on economics and law, and a wide variety of other topics. Life was comfortable and society was developed economically. Abram was not a peasant. Genesis 13:2 says that *"Abram was very rich in cattle, silver and gold."* It was therefore not easy to obey God's instructions and leave Ur. It meant transferring complete trust into God's hands.

God asks us to do the very same thing, which causes most of us to hesitate. It is altogether natural for creatures who are bound to this world, and who have never known anything else, to look to this world for security. Then God comes along and says, *"I want you to pull up your roots and set your eyes on another world, which you have never seen, but which I will show you as you go along! You can expect difficulties in this new world. People will misunderstand you and misjudge you, but that will be the price you must pay for the blessing."* Like Abram, we are then faced with a choice. Will we remain in the world, trusting in the "security" it offers, or take God at His word and step out in faith, transferring our trust to Him? **Faith says, "I will forsake the old way."**

I think it was Arthur Pink who asked the question, "What made Abram willing to go?" The answer is important. It is found in Acts 7:2-3: *"The God of Glory appeared unto our father, Abraham, when he was in Mesopotamia, before he dwelt in Haran, and said unto him, Get thee out of thy country, and from thy kindred, and come into the land which I shall show thee."* It began with a personal encounter. First, God revealed Himself and then Abram was willing to go. In other words, it began with a personal relationship. To set out on a life of faith without first coming to know the Lord Jesus would be disastrous. The vision would soon fade, and in any case, the exercise would be fruitless. God has to reveal Himself to us first. Faith will follow automatically. The prophet Isaiah was in the ministry for some time before he saw the Lord, high and lifted up upon His throne and surrounded by the Cherubim. But it was not until he saw the vision that he recognized his own unworthiness and volunteered to go out into an unbelieving world as the Lord's ambassador. Until we know the Lord, we will be unwilling to sever our trust in the old way and transfer our security to the new.

6. Faith says, *"I will occupy what God gives me."*

Verses 9-10:

"By faith he sojourned in the land of promise as in a foreign country, dwelling in tents with Isaac and Jacob, the heirs with him of the same promise; 10 for he waited for the city which has foundations, whose builder and maker is God."

Abram left the country in which he was born and went to live where God led him. (*"Out of – into."*) We don't live in a vacuum. We need direction in our lives. The people of Israel were later brought *out of* Egypt, in order to *go into* the Promised Land. It was not God's intention that they should wander in the wilderness for 40 years. That was the direct result of their lack of faith. They followed God out but were then afraid to follow Him in. Abram was different. He obeyed God because he trusted Him. He occupied all that God gave him.

However, we must not overlook the fact that the blessings of the land were still future when Abram responded to God's call. He did not occupy the land as a king. He lived there as an alien. He turned his back on the permanency of Ur and chose a life of transience in Canaan. He left Ur, where he was at home and accepted by his neighbors, and went to dwell where he was alone and rejected. He left Ur, where there was safety and occupied a place of danger, vulnerability, opposition and testing. And we must be prepared to do the same. God calls us out of the world (as far as our identification with its system is concerned) and asks us to occupy a new position by faith. The blessings are not yet apparent. They are still future. We, like Abram, are merely passing through. Yet the Lord says, *"All this is yours."* We will not always be aliens in a foreign land. We shall not always be under attack. One day the Lord will come back to reign, and when that happens the earth will be restored to its original beauty. At present we occupy with the eye of faith, waiting, like faithful Abram, for the fulfillment of the promise.

Revelation 5:10 tells us that the hosts of heaven sing praise to the Lamb and say, *"(You) have made us unto our God kings and priests: and we shall reign upon the earth."* We may not feel much like kings and priests now, but one day that will all change. Today we walk, like Abram, with tomorrow in view, trusting the unchangeable promises of God.

7. Faith says: "*I will stand upon God's promises*

Verse 11:

"By faith Sarah herself also received strength to conceive seed, and she bore a child when she was past the age, because she judged Him faithful who had promised."

If you are following the NIV translation I am afraid you will find this passage missing because the NIV translators elected to follow a minority text which omitted it. The King James, the New King James and the New American Standard Bible all preserve the reading of the majority text.

The story itself is familiar enough. Genesis 17 records that God came to Abraham and told him that He would give him a son by Sarah, who was ninety years old. Abraham misunderstood God initially and assumed God was referring to Ishmael. But the Lord confirmed His statement and told Abraham that Sarah would indeed bear a son at the appointed time and the child was to be named Isaac. God also stated that He would establish an everlasting covenant with Isaac, which would continue on to his seed after him.

This aspect of faith is extremely important. There is nothing theoretical about it. As the result of her faith, Sarah gave birth to a child in her old age. It was a tangible, practical evidence of God's power and faithfulness. As she daily held Isaac in her arms and nurtured him to manhood over a period of many years, she saw with her own eyes the physical result of her faith.

Sarah conceived the baby naturally. The process was the same for her as it is for any other woman, the world over. There is nothing unusual about women conceiving and bearing children. The unusual aspect of this case was Sarah's age. In other words, as the result of her faith, she received from God the ability to do what *for her* was impossible. "*By faith, Sarah received the STRENGTH to receive seed.*" That which amounted to a miracle for her was normal living for those around her, which tells us something about the miracles of God. They are tailor-made. They are individual in nature. That which may be normal for you might well be a miracle for me.

Just as God changed Sarah from one who was barren to one who was fruitful, so He changes men and women today. When we place our trust in Him, He enables us to do things we could never have done in our own strength. We knew a young woman in England who suffered from a serious speech impediment. She had difficulty putting two words together in normal conversation. Yet she would stand up on what we called "Preachers' Rock" during our Sunday evening services on the sea front and give her testimony in clear flowing words. To her, that was a miracle and the Lord was glorified by it.

We read in Genesis 18 that when the Lord told Abraham that Sarah would bear a child, she laughed. What did she laugh at? She laughed at the promise of God because her own weakness dominated her thinking. The Lord put His finger on her "personal inability" and said she would do what she knew she could not do. She was painfully aware of her inability to perform. Sarah laughed at herself. It was not that she didn't want a child. That had been her greatest desire all along. But she examined the evidence and evaluated the credibility of God's promise, not on the basis of His power, but on the basis of her own weakness. She was too old. That woman over there could do it. She was young and fruitful, but not Sarah. Sarah didn't have the ability to carry out God's promise! I wonder how often we think like that. Sarah was looking in the wrong direction. She was looking inward instead of upward. God does not base His promises on any ability in us. He performs His promises because He is God.

However, despite Sarah's weaknesses, she received strength to conceive seed. God said, *"At the time appointed I will come to you"* The miracle was all His. If He had not promised a child to Sarah, it would have been presumptuous of her to expect one. Faith without promise equals presumption. People sometimes claim that God is going to do this or that simply because they have claimed it by faith. But unless God has promised it, they have no basis for such a claim. Satan attempted to get Jesus to presume in this way, by throwing Himself from the pinnacle of the temple and trusting God to save Him. But Jesus said *"No!"* *"It is written, Thou shalt not tempt the Lord thy God."*

"Obviously Sarah eventually understood that the promise of God had nothing to do with her ability or inability, and in due time the child was born. Her faith was rewarded. Similarly, we must stand upon the promises of God, without looking at ourselves. The more we concentrate on ourselves, the weaker our faith will become. God is not limited by our weakness. In fact, when the promise is fulfilled our personal inability brings glory to Him. If we could perform it in our own strength, why would we need God? He is glorified when it is evident that He alone can bring about the fulfillment of His Word.

8. Faith says, "*I will stand upon the promises of God.*"

Verses 12-16:

"*Therefore from one man, and him as good as dead, were born as many as the stars of the sky in multitude - innumerable as the sand which is by the seashore. 13 These all died in faith, not having received the promises, but having seen them afar off, were assured of them, embraced them, and confessed that they were strangers and pilgrims on the earth. 14 For those who say such things declare plainly that they seek a homeland. 15 And truly if they had called to mind that country from which they had come out, they would have had opportunity to return. 16 But now they desire a better, that is, a heavenly country. Therefore God is not ashamed to be called their God, for He has prepared a city for them.*"

The Patriarchs wandered in a land which was not yet theirs, yet they believed the promises of God and trusted them. During their earthly life they did not receive the promises, but they never stopped believing and knew that one day these promises would be literally fulfilled. In his commentary on Hebrews, Arthur Pink wrote: "The Greek word for "received" signifies the actual participation in and possession of. A large part of the life of faith consists in laying hold of, and enjoying, the things promised, before the actual possession of them is obtained. It is by meditating upon and extracting their sweetness that the soul is fed and strengthened. The present spiritual happiness of the Christian consists more in promises and expectant anticipation than in actual possession, for "faith is the substance of things hoped for, the evidence of things not seen."

Abraham and his heirs were in the land but they did not belong there.

Nor did they belong any more in the land they had left. Otherwise they might have returned there. They considered themselves to be sojourners, trusting God for the final homeland, where they would truly belong, and they recognized that homeland would be a heavenly one. Consequently, we are told, *"God prepared for them a city."*

Like them, we also do not belong in this world. God's creation is beautiful and He has given it to us to enjoy, but only for a brief while. As Philippians 3:20 says, *"Our citizenship is in Heaven; from which also we look for the Savior, the Lord Jesus Christ."* Like the Patriarchs, we are sojourners, pilgrims, and we should not put down too many roots here. For the present, we walk by faith. We press forward, straining our eyes for a glimpse of the glory to come; straining our ears for the sound of the trumpet and the voice of the archangel.

9.   Faith says, *"I will put God first."*

We are thinking in terms of priorities here. What, or who, takes precedence over other considerations when we are faced with decisions? The answer to that question will determine the quality of our Christian experience and the success of our walk with the Lord. The subject of priorities is not one from which we can withdraw. We cannot choose to remain neutral. That option is not open to us. We all have priorities in our lives and we all exercise them, simply because we cannot put more than one thing in first place. Consequently, whatever (or whoever) we place at the top of our priority list will actually control our lives.

In most computer programs there are things called "default settings." These simply amount to choices that are made by the software manufacturer, and unless you deliberately change them, by an act of your will, the computer's behavior will be governed by those settings. The decision is up to you. Similarly, when God created man, He preset the "default settings" according to His perfect knowledge of man's needs. He "set" man to have fellowship with Him and to operate in perfect harmony with His will. But man was not content to do that. He chose his own way and by a deliberate act of his will, he "changed the settings." He substituted his own wisdom and his own pleasure for those of God. As the result, he immediately began to walk in the flesh rather than in the spirit.

These settings have controlled the human race ever since. No matter how much men may desire to switch back to the manufacturer's original, they have lost the ability to do so. I feel sure that after their fall Adam and Eve spent the rest of their lives in an agony of regret, as they contemplated what they had lost as the result of their willfulness. However, when the Spirit of God convicts us of our sin and saves our soul, the ability to change the settings is given back to us. Nevertheless, the change is not automatic. We have to *decide* to walk by faith. God says, in effect, "Here I am, trust me." He gives us the ability to do so, but we have to choose. We can continue to walk by sight if we wish. Many Christians do, but they cheat themselves out of God's blessing by doing so. "Faith comes by hearing, and hearing by the Word of God." We have to be doers of the Word and not hearers only if we wish to reap the benefit of the "new settings."

It is absolutely true that when we receive Christ as our Savior, it is the Holy Spirit who makes the changes. I am not suggesting for one moment that we can change ourselves. What I am saying is that an act of volition is necessary in order to place the Lord at the top of our priority list and allow Him to control our lives.

Verses 17-19:

"By faith Abraham, when he was tested, offered up Isaac, and he who had received the promises offered up his only begotten son, 18 of whom it was said, "In Isaac your seed shall be called," 19 accounting that God was able to raise him up, even from the dead, from which he also received him in a figurative sense."

This passage, and the Genesis 22 account to which it refers, is arguably one of the most sublime examples of devotion to God ever recorded. Abraham demonstrated his faith by the act of offering up his miraculous son. "Offering up", of course, is another term for sacrifice. It always demands faith to make a real sacrifice. Webster says that sacrifice is *"the destruction or surrender of something for the sake of something else."* In order to do that, some very important decisions have to be made. We have to decide what we are willing to destroy or surrender for the sake of what. Life is full of decisions like that. What am I willing to pay in exchange for a car or a house or a magazine? How much inconvenience am I willing to endure? How much loss am I willing to suffer, in order to have, or own, any given item? In most cases there is a limit and that limit marks the *value* I place upon the item. "I would sacrifice *this* much but not *that* much in exchange for this thing." The amount we are willing to sacrifice (pay) is commonly referred to as "the price."

Most of us desire to be in God's will. I think we would all agree with that. We desire the peace which we know comes from experiencing His presence and enjoying His blessing. But that blessing does not come without a price. We have to pay for it. Again, don't misunderstand what I am saying. We cannot buy the peace of God, or His fellowship. They are not for sale. However, we still have to surrender certain precious things if we wish to enjoy them. People sometimes say, *"You don't have to give up anything to be a Christian."* I would disagree with that because there are many things that we are asked to give up. That is what repentance is all about. It would be foolish to imagine that we could continue in the old way and walk with God at the same time. We have to choose whom we will serve, whom we will place first, and that is not always as straightforward as we may think.

Peter illustrated this fact when he said to Jesus, *"Though all men shall be offended because of you, yet I will never be offended."* He meant what he said. Peter was not insincere. But later, when the price of his desire was revealed to him, he discovered that he was not ready to pay it. Later, he was ready, but not at that time. He still loved the Lord and desired to be loyal to Him, but the price was beyond the value he had subconsciously set. The price, of course, was *self.* In order to choose Christ he would have to deny himself, and he discovered, to his own dismay and shame, that instead of Christ being first on his priority list, he was there himself! Obviously this problem is not unique to Peter. In principle, few of us are above making the same mistake

Jesus said, *"If any man will come after me, let him deny himself, and take up his cross, and follow me. For whosoever will save his life shall lose it; and whosoever will lose his life for my sake shall find it."* That cuts to the heart of our relationship. Faith says, "I will put God first" but faith is often tested. A reputable manufacturer will subject its products to rigorous tests in order to ensure that they will stand up to the claims it makes for them. God does the same. He tests the faith of those He calls into leadership, not to discover for Himself how well they perform (because He already knows) but to demonstrate to the individuals themselves how strong their faith is. He tested Joshua at Jericho, Asa at Mareshah, Gideon in the valley of Moreh, Elijah by the brook, Daniel in the lions' den and Joseph in the house of Potiphah. Throughout the history of both Old and New Testaments we find instances of great testing. And He still tests today.

There is absolutely no way that Abraham could have been prepared for God's command to take Isaac up into the mountain and offer him as a sacrifice. It must have caught him completely off-guard. Such a thing would never have remotely occurred to him, yet here was God asking him to do it! Every fiber in his body must have rebelled at the idea, yet there is no record of any hesitation on his part. Let us think about what Isaac represented.

First, God called him *"Your only son."* In other words, Ishmael was discounted because he was the product of Abraham's own efforts. As far as God is concerned, the fruit of our own strength is unacceptable.

Second, he was the son of Abraham's old age. He was a miracle from God, which made him very precious.

Third, he was the son of promise, the direct fulfillment of God's Word.

Fourth, he was the key to the future fulfillment of God's covenant. God told Abraham, *"Sarah, your wife, shall bear a son, and you shall call his name Isaac: and I will establish my covenant with him, for an everlasting covenant, and with his seed after him."* How would God fulfill those promises if Abraham followed through with God's command?

Fifth, he was the son of grace. He was God's idea, not Abraham's invention. Abraham could not have dreamed up a story like the one which had unfolded in his life. It was God's idea from beginning to end. Isaac was more than a son. He was the miraculous demonstration of God's sovereignty and power. The question now confronting Abraham was *"will the gift be placed higher on the list of values than the giver?"* In many cases it is. Everything we have is given to us by God. Paul asked the Corinthians, *"What have you that you did not receive?"* The answer is "nothing!" Our abilities, talents, opportunities, life, breath and intellect are all His. They are given to us as a trust and are to be used as He pleases. In Daniel's words, He is *"the God in whose hand your breath is and whose are all our ways."* He is the Giver, the Source, and sooner or later we have to decide which is more important – the Giver or His gifts.

Abraham might reasonably have responded to God's command by complaining that by offering up Isaac he would be undoing God's own promises. But he didn't. He knew that God was wiser than he was and knew the end from the beginning. To reason would have been to question God's omniscience. God knew who Isaac was. He knew what His own promise said. There was nothing that Abraham could tell God that God did not already know. Not only is God omniscient but He is right! Faith believes this, bows to it and does not argue. It knows that any request God makes has two unchanging factors: it is right and it is for the ultimate good of the one of whom God is asking it.

Abraham, in faith, went ahead and put God first. Without argument or challenge, he followed instructions. He could not tell how things would work out but, as we are told in Hebrews 11:19, he believed *"that God was able to raise him (Isaac) up, even from the dead, from which he also received him in a figurative sense."* We know the end of the story, don't we? But Abraham did not. All he knew was that God had to be right and that somehow He would work things out. Otherwise, He would break His own covenant.

In God's record, Abraham went through with the sacrifice. Hebrews 11:17 is clear: *"By faith Abraham, when he was tested, offered up Isaac, and he who had received the promises offered up his only begotten son."* The fact that God rescued Isaac at the last moment had nothing to do with Abraham's obedience. He had decided to obey God, despite the agony of mind and heart which that decision must have cost him, and God recorded it as the finished act.

Obviously the likelihood of our being tested to the degree that Abraham was tested is almost zero, but the principle is clear. God puts His finger on something very important to us and asks us to give it up for Him. He already knows where our priorities lie but He wants us to see their reality for ourselves. Do we value the gift above the Giver? As an example, I have spoken to many people in Christian service, who were offered a "plum job" just at the time God called them to serve Him. I was, and I have been surprised to discover how many others have shared my experience. It was almost as if God says, "Look, this is what you could have if you remained in the world, but I want you to leave it and follow me." The same challenge can come in many forms. The "precious" thing need not be a career. It could be a plan, security, comfort, even a person. But the principle is the same in each case. Will we choose the gift above the Giver?

It is worth repeating that God does not test us to find out anything about us. He knows everything already. The testing is to show us what is there. God was not strengthened by Abraham's faith but Abraham was. We don't know how weak or how strong our faith is until it is tested. Sometimes we need to go back to the drawing board. We are disappointed because we fail. But God is not disappointed. He is neither disappointed nor surprised by our failures. He knew all about us before we were born. He is in the business of teaching us about ourselves, and about Him. Our job is to learn the lessons He teaches us.

10. Faith says, *"I will trust God to work out His own program."*

God formed His plan before time began. He decided the direction the world would take and then set His plan in motion. It included the creation of the physical universe and everything in it. At no time was He limited by circumstances. There is a sense, I suppose, in which the outworking of His love and purpose is limited by unbelief and willfulness, but that limitation is local and individual in nature. His general purpose moves on, regardless of man's cooperation or the lack of it. His general purpose is like a big ship, which leaves its dock and steams out on to the high seas, carrying its passenger with it. On board the ship, all kinds of activities take place. Individual dramas are played out during the voyage, but they do not prevent (or even hinder) the ship from pursuing its course. They take place as the players are being carried steadily from point A to point B. The ship's destination was decided long before the passengers came aboard.

In the spiritual realm, God's purpose is the great ship; you and I are the passengers. Day by day we wrestle with the challenges of life but all the while God's great program moves on towards its pre-determined goal. The voyage is a long one. The sea of time is very wide. You and I were born on the ship and in all probability we shall die on it, but the captain never wavers. He steers on toward His destination, which was decided before the voyage began.

However, in His sovereign grace, God chose to use men and women to work the ship, so to speak. He did not *have* to. He could have used angels, had He wished, and left us out of the action altogether. But He chose to use ordinary men and women instead, frail people who make mistakes; men and women like you and me. And because we are ordinary and frail, we tend to get the wrong impression of the role we are called upon to play. We tend to imagine that the success of God's program depends on us, and that if we were taken off the ship the voyage would somehow come to an end. But that is not true. Faith says, "God will work out His own program."

Verses 20-22:

"By faith Isaac blessed Jacob and Esau concerning things to come. 21 By faith Jacob, when he was dying, blessed each of the sons of Joseph, and worshiped, leaning on the top of his staff. 22 By faith Joseph, when he was dying, made mention of the departure of the children of Israel, and gave instructions concerning his bones."

Here are three famous characters (Isaac, Jacob and Joseph) all of whom had one thing in common: they eventually came to the end of themselves. During their lifetimes, God used them to further His plan. Each of them, in turn, played his part and their stories were eternally recorded in the Scriptures. Each eventually came to the end of his role and passed from the stage of history. Others then took their place and carried on the narrative. So here, grouped together, are three dying men, each placing his trust in the integrity and power of God to fulfill His promises after they had departed. Isaac died in Hebron, a wanderer in a land that had been promised but not yet given. Jacob and Joseph both died in Egypt, not even on promised soil. However, they all died in faith, believing that God's great ship of purpose would sail on and reach its destination.

As a man, Isaac was disappointing. He betrayed weaknesses that would not normally be associated with a great man of the faith. The story of his early dealings with his twin sons, Jacob and Esau, is well known. Before the boys were born, God clearly decreed that each would found a nation and that the younger would have the preeminence. Isaac, however, favored the elder twin and clearly intended to bestow the blessing on him in violation of God's ruling. By deceit his wife, Rebekah and his younger son, Jacob, contrived a scheme to frustrate Isaac's plan, and Isaac, who had become blind, blessed Jacob by mistake.

However, having been tricked into doing the right thing, Isaac demonstrated his faith by saying, "*I have blessed him, yes, and he shall be blessed.*" That was the language of faith. God had overruled his intentions but he now submitted to the Lord's ruling, even though it was not what he had wished. Proverbs 19:21 reads: "*There are many devices in a man's heart: nevertheless the counsel of the Lord shall stand.*" Having made his decision, Isaac then trusted the Lord to work things out according to His plan.

Next, the scene switches to Jacob, now in the sunset of his years. Having lost and then found his son, Joseph, Jacob and his family had settled in Egypt, where Joseph now held high office. The land of Goshen, which had been allotted to Jacob, was pleasant and fruitful, but Jacob knew that his family would not live there permanently. He knew God had given them the land of Canaan and he was confident that God would bring his program to completion. Therefore, he called his family to him and gave them his parting message.

"*And Jacob said to Joseph, God Almighty appeared to me at Luz in the land of Canaan, and blessed me. 4 And He said to me, Behold, I will make you fruitful, and multiply you, and I will make of you a multitude of people; and I will give this land to your descendents after you for an everlasting possession.*" (Genesis 48:3-5)

"*And Israel said to Joseph, Behold, I am dying: but God shall be with you, and bring you back to the land of your fathers.*" (Genesis 48:21)

God had an unalterable plan and Jacob believed with all his heart that the plan would be fulfilled. Many years previously God had outlined the future of Israel for his grandfather, Abraham. Genesis 15:13-14 records God's words on that occasion:

"Know for sure that your seed shall be a stranger in a land that is not theirs, and shall serve them; and they shall afflict them four hundred years; 14 and also that nation, whom they shall serve, I will judge: and afterwards they shall come out with great substance."

Undoubtedly Jacob knew of this decree but whether or not he associated God's words to his present situation is open to question. The Egyptians were friendly while Joseph lived. It was later, when *"there arose a new king over Egypt, who knew not Joseph"* that Israel's trouble began. Therefore Jacob may not have connected God's statement to his family's position. Even if he had done so, he could have had no conception of the plagues which Moses would one day call down upon the land, nor the parting of the Red Sea or the forty years of wandering in the Sinai wilderness. Mercifully, that information was denied him. What he did know was that God's great ship would continue to sail on the course set for it and that no matter how complicated things might become on its decks, or in its cabins, it would move on toward its appointed goal and nothing could prevent it from reaching its destination.

From Jacob we turn now to Joseph. His story is full of parallels and analogies to the Christian life. More than any other Old Testament character, he embodied a picture of the Lord Jesus. His faithfulness to God, under the most difficult and discouraging circumstances, earned him great blessing in the land of Egypt. However, like his father, he was unshakeable in his confidence that God's future plans would be carried to fruition. His people would not always dwell in Egypt. He believed that God would one day lead them out and they would inherit the Promised Land. A long road stretched ahead, full of adversity, yet the ship would sail on unhindered.

The last verses of Genesis record Joseph's dying wish. *"And Joseph said to his brethren, I die; and God will surely visit you, and bring you out of this land into the land which He swore to Abraham, to Isaac and to Jacob. 25 And Joseph took an oath of the children of Israel, saying, God will surely visit you, and you shall carry my bones up hence."*

In each case, faith was the key. Originally, God promised the land to Abraham. In faith, Abraham passed the covenant to Isaac, his son, and in faith Isaac passed it on to his son, Jacob. Still in faith, Jacob passed it on to his son, Joseph. After Joseph died, successive generations served the Egyptians as slaves for 400 years, but trust in God's promise lived on. As succeeding generations lived and died, it was passed on by faith to their children, until one day Moses was born. Under Moses, the first stage of God's plan for Israel was fulfilled.

11. Faith says, "*I will not be afraid of men.*"

Verse 23:

"By faith Moses, when he was born, was hidden three months by his parents, because they saw he was a beautiful child; and they were not afraid of the king's command."

Not all fear is bad. Some forms are beneficial. For instance, Noah was "*moved by fear*" to build the ark. Fear of consequences may protect us from things which could cause us harm. As an example, it is good to fear being hit by a train at an open crossing because it causes us to stop and look both ways. It is when fear prevents us from doing the right thing that it becomes a problem, and it is this kind of fear that faith is designed to overcome. Fearlessness, without dependence upon the Lord is foolishness. It amounts to a dependence upon self, which is never reliable. It is the power of God that makes the difference. The fear that prevents us from doing what we should do never comes from Him.

Even the greatest men in history have experienced fear at times. Apprehension comes naturally to us all. Joshua's natural feeling of fear had to be dealt with when he was called to lead the nation. God said, "*Be strong and of a good courage, be not afraid, neither be thou dismayed, for the Lord your God is with you wherever you go.*" Later, when God called Jeremiah into the ministry, the prophet's natural fear surfaced. Again, God's remedy was to assure him of His presence. He said, "*Be not afraid of their faces; for I am with you to deliver you.*" The ability to overcome anxiety is always found in the assurance that God is present and in control.

Here in verse 23 there are actually two groups of people who demonstrated the victory of faith over fear. In Exodus 1:15-16 we are told that the king of Egypt instructed the midwives to kill the Hebrew male babies but save the girls alive. There were obviously many midwives in Egypt but two are spotlighted in this narrative. Their names were Shiphra and Puah. They were faced with a choice. Either they would obey Pharaoh and displease God or they would obey God and displease Pharaoh. They could not do both. Nobody had to tell them that Pharaoh's command was against God's principles (just as you and I know instinctively what is right and what is wrong). The problem is that deciding to do what is right may sometimes cause repercussions which we would rather not risk. It is here that fear of consequences could prevent us from being true to our conscience.

In the case of Shiphra and Puah, their decision to defy Pharaoh's edict involved considerable danger, possibly even death, but fortunately for Moses, these Hebrew midwives had the courage of their convictions. They did what was right, even though they knew the danger. Exodus 1:17 tells us that the reason for their courage was that *"they feared God."* The result of their bravery was not only that Moses was born alive but that God protected them, blessed them and increased their own families.

The second group mentioned in verse 23 is, of course, the parents of Moses, whose names were Amram and Jochabed (Numbers 26:59). The midwives did their part and the parents did theirs. When Pharaoh saw that the midwives were uncooperative he commanded his own people to throw any male Hebrew child they found into the Nile. No doubt some little ones perished in this way. This command posed an even greater danger because the average Egyptian possessed neither the courage nor the ethics of the Hebrew midwives. So why were Moses' parents unafraid? Upon what was their faith founded? It was founded upon perception. They perceived that God had something special planned for their child. They did not base their faith on the fact that Moses was good to look at. What parent does not think that of their child? The KJV and the NASB both say that Moses was *"a beautiful child."* However, they both miss the sense. Due to form, the NIV does not translate the phrase but paraphrases it, and in doing so, captures the best picture. It says that Moses *"was no ordinary child."* Acts 7:20 helps us by stating that the child, Moses, was *"lovely in the sight of God."* (NASB). The KJV says he was *"exceeding fair"* but adds *" fair unto God"* in the margin. His parents discerned that God had a purpose for Moses. Both groups, midwives and parents alike, demonstrated their faith by perceiving God's will and following it, regardless of the outcome. Faith says, *"I will not be afraid."*

12. Faith says, *"**I will choose God's way**."*

Verses 24-26:

"By faith Moses, when he became of age, refused to be called the son of Pharaoh's daughter, 25 choosing rather to suffer affliction with the people of God than to enjoy the passing pleasures of sin, 26 esteeming the reproach of Christ greater riches than the treasures in Egypt; for he looked to the reward."

Usually we think of faith as being positive. We *"go forth"* by faith, *"walk"* by faith, or *"overcome"* by faith. However, sometimes faith has to be used in a negative form, as it was here. *"Moses refused by faith."* Once again, we see the principle of choice in action. Moses evaluated the alternatives and chose to refuse a privilege that was offered to him. Choice is always a privilege, but along with the choice comes responsibility. We all know about the principle of sowing and reaping. That is a law of nature. The trouble with society today is that people want to be free to sow the wrong seed (because the process is pleasant and appeals to the flesh) but they don't want to accept responsibility for the outcome. Sowing the right seed is a matter of choice. Nobody forces us to sin. (If they tried, we would probably stubbornly refuse to sin on principle). We *choose* to sin, or we choose not to sin, as the case may be.

Moses made a choice. He refused something very attractive. He refused to be called the son of Pharaoh's daughter. He had been raised from the age of three months in Pharaoh's palace. His mother had acted as his nursemaid initially but eventually he was brought to Pharaoh's daughter and his formal education began. Acts 7:22 tells us that *"Moses was learned in all the wisdom of the Egyptians and was mighty in word and deed."* He had a lot going for him. For forty years he was groomed for Egyptian leadership. He had never known anything else. He had never made bricks and had never been a slave. Had he wished, he could have remained in Pharaoh's palace and become a very powerful prince.

It would have been so easy for Moses to rationalize. *"God put me here and must intend for me to stay." " It would be silly to give up this opportunity." "Maybe I should use my influence to help my people."* But Moses knew that his people would not remain in Egypt indefinitely. They were going to leave Egypt. How did he know? Perhaps his mother taught him during his early years. In any case, God's ancient promise to Abraham must have been widely known and taught among the Hebrew people. Moses was obviously good at arithmetic and he knew that the time for Israel's departure was drawing near, though he had no idea how the departure would be accomplished. He had a choice to make. Either he could identify with God's people and lose the favor of Pharaoh, or he could remain where he was, claim his position in the palace, and forfeit the promise which God had given to Abraham centuries previously. In addition, if he chose the second alternative he would become part of that which God had promised to judge.

This principle is still true today. The world is heading for judgment. It is doomed; nothing can prevent the judgment from taking place. We can either cling to the world system or break from it. Clinging to it would be like refusing to leave a sinking ship. There may have been doubts in Moses' mind. Suppose he was wrong about the timing of God's promise? After all, the promise had been made approximately six hundred years previously. (The equivalent today would be to look back to a promise made in the 1400's, when the Tudor kings occupied the throne of England). Suppose Moses had misinterpreted God's words? But he acted on faith and sometimes we, too, need to be adventurous in our service for the lord.

When you find yourself questioning or doubting the decisions you made in faith, remember Moses between his 40th and 80th birthdays. He stepped out in faith and experienced hard times as the result. For 40 years this prince kept sheep in the wilderness, a fugitive from his home in Egypt, while his people continued to live in slavery. God could not use him immediately. Moses had to be trained in the school of experience. But eventually, in God's own time, he became a major cog in the great wheel of God's purpose. As verse 25 tells us, he chose *"rather to suffer affliction with the people of God than to enjoy the passing pleasures of sin."* It seems to me that Egypt and sin are used as synonyms here. As far as we can tell, Moses did not engage in anything particularly sinful while in the palace of Pharaoh, but being where you know God does not want you to be amounts to almost the same thing. Moses knew instinctively that he did not belong in Egypt. He was a man out of place – a good man in a bad place. God was not on Egypt's side and being involved with anything that does not carry God's approval amounts to sin. To enjoy the pleasures of Pharaoh's court, while knowing that he should not be there was, to Moses, sin.

Verse 26 raises a question. *"esteeming the reproach of Christ greater riches than the treasures in Egypt; for he looked to the reward."*

Obviously, Moses, the man, knew nothing about Christ. The Lord's atoning death outside the city walls was still fifteen hundred years in the future. Yet in John 5:46 Jesus said, *"Had you believed Moses, you would have believed me; for he wrote of me."* And on the Emmaus road, as Jesus walked with His disciples, we are told that *"beginning at Moses and all the prophets, (He) expounded unto them in all the Scriptures, the things concerning Himself."* Moses had no knowledge of the historical Jesus but he understood the reproach Jesus eventually bore, as the price of saving his people. He counted the same price for the same reason and chose to pay it.

The treasures of Egypt were considerable but physical treasure is often found in the wrong places. Following his conscience, Moses turned away from gain to follow what he knew God was calling him to do. Being faithful sometimes leads to hardship but faith takes the long view. God doesn't always reward his children immediately. Moses waited many years for his reward. He chose to suffer hardship under the approval of God, rather than live at ease under God's judgment. He looked away to the future and remembered the bones of Joseph, waiting to be carried out. He was determined to leave Egypt with them.

13. Faith says, ***"I will not be afraid of the judgment of God."***

Verses 27-28:

"By faith he forsook Egypt, not fearing the wrath of the king; for he endured as seeing Him who is invisible. 28 By faith he kept the Passover and the sprinkling of blood, lest he who destroyed the firstborn should touch them."

At this point we switch from the faith of one person to the collective faith of the nation which he led. As we do so, we must recognize that within that nation there was a cross-section of human nature, just as there is in our nation today. Not all the people were brave, not all were strong in their spiritual lives and, as far as their thoughts, words and deeds were concerned, not all the people were righteous. All the temperaments were represented and many different experiences combined to make these two-million-odd people what they were. They were ordinary folks, just like you and me. They each had their hang-ups, strengths and weaknesses. Some were optimists and others were pessimists, yet by faith they collectively escaped the judgment of God. Together, they overcame an impossible barrier which barred their escape from Egypt and witnessed God's miraculous actions on their behalf.

Many barriers barred their entrance into the Promised Land. Some were spiritual, as in the case of the Passover, others were natural, such as the flooded Jordan valley, and still others were man-made, such as Jericho, yet all of these barriers were overcome by God in response to faith. As is so often the case, they were vanquished, not by noble words but by acts of obedience. In each instance, the people simply did as they were told, even though they did not understand the reasons for the action. They followed instructions and trusted God to do the rest, and each time God came through on their behalf. This illustrates two principles, first, faith demands action before it becomes operative and second, the action must be in obedience to the revealed Word of God. For instance, I might try to balance across a wire stretched between two buildings. This would require a huge amount of faith on my part, but it would not be faith in God because God has not told me to do it. Faith in God must always be preceded by His instructions, which are found in His Word.

Verse 27 refers to the exodus from Egypt itself. Even if Moses was unafraid during the process, we can rest assured that many among the people were afraid, especially when they saw the Egyptian cavalry coming after them! However, they did not break ranks and run. They followed instructions and continued on their way. We saw that faith is a choice and the people of Israel chose to trust God rather than their own emotions. In consequence God saw them safely across the watery barrier that stood between them and freedom.

Verse 28 speaks of the Passover (Exodus 12:12-28). Its name comes from the fact that the judgment of God passed over the descendents of Israel and left them unharmed, while the people of Egypt suffered its full force. The judgment was very real and Israel was warned that at a specific day and time it would fall, whether they were ready or not. Israel had no specific merit. The Hebrew people were no better than the Egyptians. God's grace was demonstrated, not by excluding Israel from Judgment, because He did not. It was demonstrated in the fact that He provided them with a means of escape, through the blood of the lamb. They could have discounted God's warning, or they could have just failed to follow His instructions. Either decision would have resulted in death. However, in obedience to God's instructions, the people killed the lamb, applied its blood to the doorposts of their tents and waited inside for the judgment to pass over them. As the result, they were saved, whereas the Egyptians were not. I believe that, had the Egyptians heard God's instructions and followed them in faith, they also would have been saved. It was not the Israelite's nationality that saved them, but their obedience to the Word of God.

We should always remember that the final judgment of this age has also been decided. The date and time are already set, even though only God knows when that will be. It will come, whether we are ready or not. God has no favorites. The Scriptures tell us that "*there is no respect of persons with Him.*" By grace, He has provided a way of escape, which is the Lord Jesus Christ, who, as the Lamb of God, shed His blood on the cross to pay for our sin. Provided we are sheltering beneath that fact, as the ancient Israelites did on the night of the Passover, we need have no fear of the judgment. Our faith, like theirs, must not be in ourselves, in our ability to understand or in our knowledge of the Scriptures. It must rest totally in the promises of God and the sacrifice of Jesus Christ.

Many believers still fear the judgment. They imagine that they will still have to stand before the Great White Throne and answer for their sin. But that is not what the Bible teaches. If we have truly trusted in the finished work of the Savior, we shall never have to stand before the judgment throne because Christ stood there in our place and answered for our sins. 1 John 4:17 says, *"Herein is our love made perfect, that we may have boldness in the Day of Judgment: because as He is, so are we in this world."* How is He in this world? He is perfect and free from sin. Because we are in Him, we are considered by God to be *"as He is"* (without sin). Jude records that we shall be presented *"faultless before the presence of His glory with exceeding joy."* Faith says, "I will not be afraid of the judgment of God."

14. Faith says, *"I will trust God to remove all obstacles."*

Verse 29:

"By faith they passed through the Red Sea as by dry land, whereas the Egyptians, attempting to do so, were drowned."

Exodus 14:1-14 tells us the dramatic story of Israel's deliverance from Egypt. Three things stand out in the account. First, the problem was real, second, the people were unable to do anything about it, and third, God was committed to help them. He gave the people precise instructions concerning their position, including where to camp prior to the crossing. It did not seem like a good camping site. Most human generals would have rejected it out of hand. It was entangled by the land, shut in by the wilderness and cut off by the sea! The one important factor was that God placed them there.

Someone might say, "Yes, I understand their story, but my case is different. I am so weak. I have so little faith. I have so many doubts!" Maybe so, but does what we read in Exodus 14:10-12 sound like "great faith?"

"And when Pharaoh drew nigh, the children of Israel lifted up their eyes, and, behold, the Egyptians marched after them; and they were sore afraid: and the children of Israel cried out to the Lord. 11 And they said to Moses, because there were no graves in Egypt, have you taken us away to die in the wilderness? Why have you dealt thus with us, to carry us forth out of Egypt? 12 Is this not

the word we told you in Egypt, saying, leave us alone, that we may serve the Egyptians? For it would have been better for us to serve the Egyptians, than to die in the wilderness."

These people did not display great faith; they did not sound like giants of confidence; their composure in the face of trouble was not impressive. They panicked and blamed Moses for everything. Yet Hebrews 11:29 records, *"By faith they passed through the Red Sea."* The key comes in the following verses. Moses' message had two parts, one for the people and one concerning God. Regarding God, he said (Exodus 14:13): *"He will show you"*, *"He will fight for you"*, *"Salvation is His."* To the people he said, *"Fear not"*, *"Stand still"*, *"See"*, *"Hold your peace."* All the action belonged to God. The people were to be entirely passive. They were even commanded to be quiet!

God then said, *"Why do you cry to me? Tell the children of Israel to go forward."* Where to? Into the sea, of course! That sounded like a ridiculous order. We know how the story worked out but the Israelites had to find out as they went along. That is always the way it is. God never tells us the outcome of a problem in advance. He expects us to go forward and trust Him to work out the details. Usually we see God's solutions clearest when we look back. Things often don't make sense at the time – to us. But God knows precisely what He is doing and, if we are willing to trust Him, we shall see His hand at work.

Verse 30:

"By faith the walls of Jericho fell down after they were encircled for seven days."

Like the Red Sea, the walls of Jericho were not a theoretical barrier. They were real walls, made of real stone. In fact, they were double. There was an inner wall, twelve feet thick, then a space of fifteen feet and then an outer wall, six feet in thickness. It was about the strongest barrier man could devise at the time. It seemed as if the enemy held the ace card. It often seems like that. But we know the famous story -- how the people, led by the priests, walked round and round the city and how, at the blast of trumpets and a great shout from the people, the walls fell down flat. God said, *"I have given Jericho into your hand."* But when He spoke, the wall still stood. There was no outward evidence to back up His statement. No cracks could be seen, no rumbles heard, no smoke rising from within the city. The place looked as strong as ever, but the statement had been made, and with God that is as good as the completed action. All the people had to do was walk around the place and shout! God did the rest. As Paul wrote to the Corinthians, *"For though we walk in the flesh, we do not war in the flesh. For the weapons of our warfare are not carnal, but mighty through God, for the pulling down of strongholds."* (2 Corinthians 10:3-5)

Times have not changed very much. Many obstacles still stand in our way as we walk this life and some of them seem insurmountable. However, with God all things are possible. Just as He overcame the Red Sea, the Jordan River in flood and the walls of Jericho, so He still possesses His ancient power. If we trust Him, He will see us through. Faith says, "I will trust God to remove all obstacles."

15. Faith says, *"I will identify with God's people."*

Verse 31:

"By faith the harlot Rahab did not perish with those who did not believe, when she had received the spies with peace."

Here we have quite a change of scenery. Abraham was a man of dignity when God called him. Moses grew up in the palace of a king. Isaac, Jacob and Joseph were heirs of great wealth and blessing, but Rahab was at the bottom of the pile. She was a prostitute, a woman of the streets. Nobody would have expected her to rise to the hall of fame, yet she has gone down in history, not only as a great example of faith but as the great grandmother of King David, and a vital link in the family line of the Lord Jesus Himself.

Rahab is said to have demonstrated faith when she *"received the spies with peace."* As the result, when Jericho was destroyed, she *"perished not with those who did not believe."* However, a reading of Joshua 2:1-24 and 6:21-25 clarifies that the story contained more than Rahab's hospitality. First, when officials were sent to her door demanding that she hand over the two men whom Joshua had sent into Jericho to spy out the land, she hid them and protected them from arrest. She did this at considerable personal danger. Obviously, something more than compassion for strangers motivated her. This was revealed a few verses later, when she said to the men:

> *"I know that the Lord has given you the land, and that your terror has fallen upon us, and that all the inhabitants of the land faint because of you. For we have heard how the Lord dried up the waters of the Red Sea for you, when you came out of Egypt, and what He did to the two kings of the Amorites, that were on the other side of Jordan, Sihon and Og, whom you utterly destroyed. And as soon as we had heard these things, our hearts did melt, neither did there remain any more courage in any man, because of you: for the Lord your God, He is God of heaven above and earth beneath."* (Joshua 2:9-11)

The Canaanite's fear began when the Lord parted the Red Sea. That was forty years before Israel arrived at Jericho. Throughout that time the Canaanites had feared the approach of Israel, but their fear had evidently not resulted in faith. They were terrified of Israel but had not recognized that it was God, rather than Israel, whom they should fear. Rahab alone had transferred her fear to the Lord and understood that it was His great power that brought the invading force to her land. When the opportunity arose for her to demonstrate her faith, she lost no time in doing so. As the result, she and her entire family were saved when the city fell.

Rahab did not have much to offer. Her faith was a very imperfect thing. Nevertheless, she could see that God, through His people, was going to be victorious and she wanted to be part of the victory. She looked back over 40 years of history to Israel's miraculous rescue from Egypt. It had happened before she was born but she had heard the story from others and she had applied its lessons to her own generation. There is often a reluctance to do this today.

We also should be able to read the evidence of God's power in past generations and apply its truth to the present day, yet this is rarely done. The same mistakes are repeated over and over again and we wonder why things don't work out better than they do. Rahab was a rare exception. She was a person who thought for herself, decided for herself what she believed, and did not go along with the tide of popular thinking. She lived in a heathen society. In order to embrace God's cause she had no alternative but to turn her back on the system she had always known. She could not keep both. She had to choose, and she chose to identify with God's side in the battle.

Rahab could have chosen to be popular with those around her. She would have died with them had she done so. It was a difficult decision to make. She would have been branded as a traitor had her secret leaked out. As it is, Rahab has been criticized through the centuries because she sided with the enemy. But that depends on one's point of view. The spies were "bad" to those in Jericho because they represented the opposing side. Yet they were under the hand of God and that which is in His perfect will can hardly be termed "bad". God's Spirit is in opposition to the ways of the society in which we live. He stands for its destruction but that does not make Him "bad." "Goodness" and "badness" depend on which side we wish to support.

Left to ourselves, our hearts are *straitly shut up*", just like Jericho was in the days of Joshua and Rahab. God's Spirit comes along and "slips in" unaware, and we have to decide which side we are on. The scarlet thread, upon which Rahab relied, was undetected by the inhabitants around her. If they saw it, they had no idea what is signified. They had no comprehension of the relationship she now enjoyed with the forces of God. In the same way, the world has no comprehension of the relationship that exists between God and the surrendered human heart.

Some say that Rahab "sold" the city, but she did not. The people sold themselves by their sin. Judgment was approaching anyway. Rahab did not speed Jericho's fall. In a sense, she delayed it because Joshua made no move until the spies returned with their report. The people of Jericho had access to the same information that Rahab had. They also knew of the greatness of God's power in behalf of Israel. They had heard the same stories of Israel's progress. However, they failed to translate what they heard into belief. They resisted God's cause. They shut up their city, just like people shut up their hearts today. They trembled, but wanted nothing to do with God's people. By contrast, Rahab made her choice and all the power of Israel was brought to bear on her rescue.

The spies' visit had no bearing on the fall of Jericho. They took back no information that affected the final outcome of the battle. The only thing that was achieved was Rahab's protection. In effect, two million people were kept waiting until the welfare of Rahab was secured. God changed her from a poor despised prostitute into the mother of Boaz, the mother-in-law of Ruth, the great grandmother of King David and a direct ancestor of the Lord Jesus Christ! Why? Because she chose to identify with God's people in the battle and to trust God for her salvation.

The writer to the Hebrews now moves from the particular to the general. Until this point, he has concentrated on specific individuals as illustrations of faith in action. He has picked them out of the many and placed them under the microscope, in order to teach us how faith works under pressure. There are many examples from which to choose. The Bible is full of them. But now, from verse 32 onwards, he moves very rapidly over the general history of Israel, leaving his readers to fill in the details.

Verse 32:

"And what more shall I say? For the time would fail me to tell of Gideon and Barak and Samson and Jephthah, also of David and Samuel and the prophets

Verse 32 mentions six people by name (Gideon, Barak, Samson, Jephthah, David and Samuel) without singling out any particular episodes in their lives. From verse 33 to the end of the chapter, he mentions none by name. Nevertheless, faith, as the central subject, never leaves the stage. These people all lived, faced their trials and overcame by faith. They have all gone down in history as victors over the power of evil, even though many died in the process. Let us go quickly through the list and take a snapshot of each individual as we go.

Four of the six characters are taken from the book of Judges. We read about **Gideon** in Judges 6, 7 and 8. His life is a study on its own. He started out as a timid, frightened man, thrashing wheat in a winepress for fear that the enemy might catch him if he worked on the open thrashing floor. Due to the sins of the nation, God had allowed the

Midianites to take control of the land. Despite his timidity, Gideon was called to lead the people back to victory and throw the Midianite invader out of the land. He was an unlikely candidate for heroism. He would much rather have remained out of sight and allowed someone else to be the leader. But by faith he obeyed, trusting God to do what he knew he was incapable of doing himself. With only three hundred men, he defeated the armies of Midian. Nor was it by force of arms that he prevailed. It was by faith alone because his men were unarmed. They faced the enemy with a trumpet in one hand and a clay pot in which was hidden a light in the other. At a given signal, the pots were smashed, the lights raised high, the trumpets blown, the men gave a great shout and the enemy fled in terror. It took enormous courage to follow God's instructions, but Gideon and his men believed God for the victory and God came through for them in a wonderful way. John wrote: *"This is the victory that overcomes the world, even our faith."*

Barak comes next. We read about him in Judges 4. He fought the forces of Sisera, the famous Canaanite general. A message came to Barak from Deborah, a prophetess, that God would give Sisera into their hand. So Barak, in obedience to God's command, went out against superior odds and overcame them. Once again, the victory was not due to Barak's abilities but in the truth that God would be as good as His word.

The life of **Samson** is recorded in Judges 13-16. It is a wild and strange account, in which Samson's own indiscipline lands him in serious trouble. Yet, despite his rebellious personality, he displayed feats of strength that could not have been performed by normal men – slaying a thousand Philistines single-handedly with an ass's jawbone, for instance, or carrying the posts and gates of Gaza on his shoulder up a steep hill, or his final act of destroying the great temple of Dagon by pushing out the pillars supporting the roof and bringing down the building on himself and his tormentors..All these feats of superhuman strength demanded faith, and, wild though he was, Samson obviously drew his phenomenal strength from God.

Jephthah is highlighted in Judges 11. He was the leader whom God raised up to rescue the people from the power of Ammon. Once again, he trusted God to give him the victory and boldly attacked the

Ammonites in the strength of faith. God gave him a mighty victory over his enemies.

Samuel and David are both featured in the books of 1 and 2 Samuel. Samuel was a priest and David was a king. Both exercised faith. Samuel called down thunder and rain on the people (a very unusual thing in that part of the world) when they demanded a king). He then anointed David while Saul still occupied the throne of Israel, because God told him to do so. That took courage, but Samuel trusted God to work out the details.

On his part, David faced Goliath of Gath with a sling and a handful of smooth stones, overcoming him in the name of the Lord of Hosts. He also resisted harming King Saul, when Saul was in his power, even though the king had vowed to kill him. David trusted God to work out the details of succession. He made his mistakes but he was a mighty warrior and led his armies to many victories.

The **prophets** also universally faced the wrath of kings and people when they spoke forth the truth of God's word to a generation that did not want to hear it. By faith, they risked life and freedom in order to obey God. They trusted Him to protect them from their adversaries. All these were men of faith. Each relied upon God when the going became tough, and each encouraged others to be bold. Their faith benefitted their people. Their victories of faith were not personal victories; they were public victories, because others were emboldened and encouraged in their own faith as they witnessed the faith of their leaders. We need people who will stand strong today, also, and dare to believe God against odds. Fearless conviction has an electrifying effect on others, who in themselves would not have the boldness to stand.

Verse 33:

"Who through faith subdued kingdoms."

Joshua and David both subdued kingdoms, not just for the purpose of extending their territory, but because those kingdoms stood in the way of God's work. God is against anything that opposes His plan, and we can resist it in faith, trusting Him for the victory.

Verse 33 again:

". . .*wrought righteousness.*"

Elijah and Elisha wrought righteousness in their time. Elijah, especially, exercised incredible faith when he defied King Ahab and challenged the priests of Baal to a contest on Mount Carmel (1 Kings 18:17-39). He did not know how his challenge would work out but his faith was so great that he deliberately dowsed the sacrifice with water several times before calling down fire from heaven to consume it.

Verse 33 again:

". . . *obtained promises.*"

Caleb was a notable example of this. Having faithfully served Moses throughout the wilderness wanderings, he came to Joshua and demanded Hebron as his inheritance. Moses had promised it to him forty years previously, when he had gone with Joshua to spy out the land. It was the land of the giants and walled cities, which had so frightened the previous generation of Israelites. That made no difference to Caleb. He said, "*Give me this mountain*" and then went on to take it by conquest because he trusted God to fulfill His promise.

Verse 33 once again:

". . . *stopped the mouths of lions.*"

This is an obvious one. By faith, Daniel spent a night in the lions' den, rather than pray to the heathen king, Darius, and God closed the lions' mouths so that they did Daniel no harm

Verse 34:

"*Quenched the violence of the fire.*"

Here is another obvious one. Shadrach, Meshach and Abed-nego chose rather to be thrown into the furnace than to worship Nebuchadnezzar's image. They openly claimed that God was able to deliver them from the flames (which, of course, He did).

Verse 34 again:

"*. . . escaped the edge of the sword.*"

Both David and Jeremiah were illustrations of this phrase. God wonderfully protected them from harm because they trusted Him for their protection.

Verse 34 again"

"*. . . out of weakness were made strong.*"

Gideon was one person who fitted with this description. Sarah was another. She "*received strength to conceive seed*" when she was past the age of child-bearing, because she believed God's promise.

Verse 34 again:

"*. . . waxed valiant in fight, turned to flight the armies of the aliens.*"

Joshua was certainly valiant in battle, and so were David, Jonathan and Barak.

Verse 35:

"*Women received their dead raised to life again.*"

Elijah and Elisha were both involved in the miraculous raising of persons who had died.

Verse 35 again"

"*And others were tortured, not accepting deliverance, that they might obtain a better resurrection.*"

Sad to say, believers have been subjected to various forms of torture throughout history, even to the present day, in an attempt to make them deny their faith. Many have prevailed and died rather than give in. Their faith has proved mightier than the agony to which they have been subjected.

Verse 36:

"Still others had trial of mockings and scourgings, yes, and of chains and imprisonment."

In the New Testament, Paul, Silas and Peter all experienced this mistreatment. No doubt Old Testament characters suffered similarly but are not mentioned by name. Joseph, of course, suffered imprisonment, but not specifically due to his beliefs. Nevertheless, he was a wonderful example of faith in action under adverse conditions.

Verses 37-38:

"They were stoned, they were sawn in two, were tempted, were slain with the sword. They wandered about in sheepskins and goatskins, being destitute, afflicted, tormented. 38 of whom the world was not worthy. They wandered in deserts and mountains, in dens and caves of the earth."

Both Stephen and Paul were stoned. Ancient tradition asserts that Isaiah was killed by being placed between two planks of wood and sawn in two. John the Baptist and Paul were both executed with the sword. We have no specific record of those who wandered, destitute, but there were certainly many who fell into this category. They all demonstrated faith in their lives. Many accounted for very little in the world's eyes. Their names are not recorded on earth but God knows who they are. They are great in His eyes because they pleased God by trusting Him.

Verses 39-40:

"And all these, having obtained a good testimony through faith, did not receive the promise, 40 God having provided something better for us, that they should not be made perfect apart from us."

Verse 39 is almost a repeat of verse 13. Despite their outstanding testimony these faithful believers, with the exception of the New Testament characters mentioned above, did not receive the promise because something stood in their way. They had to wait in Paradise (Abraham's bosom, sheol) until atonement for sin was finally made. (Luke 16:19-31). They pleased God but they still did not immediately get through to their final goal. After Jesus arose, He "*led captivity captive;*" He emptied sheol and led its occupants victoriously into heaven.

CHAPTER 12

Chapter 12 opens by stating that we are surrounded by a cloud of witnesses. The people described here in chapter 11 are these witnesses. They surround us. Chapter 11 refers to what *they* did. Chapter 12 will describe what *we* should be doing. The heroes of chapter 11 did not choose circumstances which fitted their own plans. Noah did not decide to have a flood (because he'd come across some cool plans for an ark). Abel did not invent the idea of a blood sacrifice (because he happened to have a lamb). Moses did not dream up the Passover (to impress his people). *GOD* set the race, and the witnesses demonstrated their faith by the way they faced their (unexpected) problems. They disregarded personal weakness or personal safety. In dependence upon God and in obedience to His will, they stepped out against the odds and trusted Him for the outcome.

Each individual's challenge was (and still is) very personal. It is different from everyone else's. For instance, Noah did not have to attack Jericho, Moses did not have to build an ark, Sarah did not have to receive the spies, Abraham did not have to fight Goliath, and Gideon did not have to offer up his son. Their circumstances were all unique, but the faith was the same in every case. It was *"the substance of things hoped for; the evidence on things not seen."*

The question now is "how am I to run this race which God has set before me?"

Running the race

Verse 1:

"Therefore we also, since we are surrounded by so great a cloud of witnesses, let us lay aside every weight, and the sin which so easily

ensnares us, and let us run with endurance the race that is set before us."

The Old Testament saints ran the race that was set before them; now it is our turn to follow their example. As we have seen, many of them faced challenges along the way, which might have hindered them and even caused them to give up altogether, but they trusted God to carry them through and pressed on to victory. We also face opposition, both from within and without but the weapons of our warfare are mighty through God. Provided we commit our way to the Lord, we also shall prevail.

The word translated *"weight"* means something that is crooked or hooked -- anything that by hanging onto us increases the weight we carry. An athlete preparing to run in the games would remove anything that might hinder his progress. As Christians, we also should free ourselves of anything that might obstruct our progress. Such things come in a variety of forms. It may be pride, anger, the love of money, selfishness, immorality or any number of similar characteristics that would hinder our progress. Unnecessary weight might also arise in the form of a wrong relationship or an excessive preoccupation with some amusement or occupation. Anything that could hinder our freedom to run the race is a weight – a strike against us winning through.

Paul likened himself to an Olympic athlete when he wrote 1 Corinthians 9:24-27. He said:

"Do you not know that those run in a race all run, but one receives the crown? Run in such a way that you may obtain it. 25 And everyone who competes for the prize is temperate in all things. Now they do it to obtain a perishable crown, but we for an imperishable crown. 26 Therefore I run, not with uncertainty. I fight, not as one who beats the air. 27 But I discipline my body and bring it into subjection, lest, when I have preached to others, I myself should become disqualified."

"The sin which so easily besets us" would be that into which we are most likely to fall as individuals. It would probably be different with each person. It could be the return of an old habit which we thought we had overcome. It could be an area connected with our life before conversion,

or where by nature we are vulnerable to temptation. Just as in Holland, the dykes have to be properly maintained to prevent the sea from flowing in and re-occupying the land it once covered, so believers must be aware of weak areas and keep alert to sudden attack.

The King James Bible renders the last phrase of verse 1 as "*run with patience*," but "*run with endurance*" is probably a better translation. The word literally means "*abiding under,*" which conveys the sense of accepting the race which God has assigned us and running it without complaining or giving up. The believer who bemoans the difficulty of his way is not a very good testimony.

Verses 2-3:

"*. . . looking unto Jesus, the author and finisher of our faith, who for the joy that was set before Him endured the cross, despising the shame, and has sat down at the right hand of the throne of God. 3 For consider Him who endured such hostility from sinners against Himself, lest you become weary and discouraged in your souls.*"

"*Looking unto*" is literally "*looking away.*" We are to look *away* to Jesus, which means looking away from ourselves. Our problems often press so heavily upon us that we find ourselves dwelling on them. Our attention is directed inward instead of outward, which can result in discouragement and depression. Here we are told that Jesus is "*the author and the finisher of our faith.*" Simply looking away from our problems would not solve them but fixing our gaze, our faith and dependence on the Lord Jesus will work wonders.

The wonderful truth is that we have a God in heaven who actually remembers what it feels like to go through terrible testing. When we hit difficulties, no matter what they may be, we should look away to Him. He understands. We should "*consider*" (meditate upon) Him and remember, not only what He suffered, but also His outlook as He endured the suffering. He did it "*for the joy that was set before Him*" – not in this world but in the next. Jesus knew that the eternal joy in Heaven, as the result of His redemptive work, would far surpass the temporal price He had to pay. We must remember that also. The difficulties of this life are nothing compared with the joy that is to come to those who are faithful. Paul spelled this out to the Corinthians when he wrote:

> *"For which cause we do not lose heart; but though our outward man is perishing, yet the inward man is being renewed day by day. For our light affliction, which is but for a moment, works for us a far more exceeding and eternal weight of glory."* (2 Corinthians 4:16-17).

Recognizing this truth will help us to avoid growing weary and faint hearted. There is no doubt that the race can be very hard and it is easy to become exhausted. My wife and I did a lot of cycling when we were young. There was a certain condition which was known among our group as *"the bonk."* After a long day of riding, especially against the wind, our legs would turn to jelly, cold sweat would break out on our brow and we would feel as if we were going to die. That was *"the bonk."* Rest and chocolate soon got us going again.

Of course, the race that is set before us is a spiritual exercise rather than a physical one. The exhaustion we may experience is mental or emotional in nature. It is exhaustion of the heart and mind that we must guard against because it is in the mind that we are tempted to give up. We must be careful to avoid getting mental and spiritual "bonk." Discouragement, anxiety, fear, doubt, anger and jealousy all have to do with the mind and it is in those areas that the enemy is most likely to strike. In fact, it is in those areas that the race may be won or lost.

When we become weary in our minds, Satan is right there to corrupt our thinking and make us begin to believe things about God that are not true. We may be tempted to question Him, even to become angry with Him. To safeguard against this state of affairs, we must *"consider Jesus."* What are we to consider? Well, how did He run His race? He ran it in faith, didn't He? He endured, keeping His eyes on the joy He knew was awaiting Him once He triumphed. He focused on the final goal and that is also how we should run our race.

Enduring affliction

Verse 4:

"You have not yet resisted to bloodshed, striving against sin."

The inference here is that the Christian path is a life and death struggle. Jesus ran the race set before Him and paid a fearful price. Many Christians through the centuries have been (and still are being) martyred for their faith. Because Satan hates God, he also hates all those who turn to God through the Lord Jesus Christ. He does all he can to discourage them in their faith. The only safe way to overcome his attacks is to look away to Jesus and draw from Him the strength we need. The writer to the Hebrews points out to his readers that though they may have been subjected to violent storms in their Christian lives, they had not been called upon to pay the ultimate price and should consequently fight on, keeping their eyes upon Christ.

The Lord's chastening

Verses 5-6:

"And you have forgotten the exhortation which speaks to you as to sons: "My son, do not despise the chastening of the Lord, nor be discouraged when you are rebuked by Him; 6 For whom the Lord loves He chastens, and scourges every son whom He receives."

With this passage, a new phase of teaching is introduced. The author switches from an examination of faith itself to relationships, which are very important as we run the race of life. Relationships help to carry us through our difficulties and assist us in negotiating the obstacles confronting us along the way. The passage itself contains a rough quotation from Proverbs 3:11-12, and refers to the normal relationship between father and son. If it is a good relationship it will produce stability and confidence in the next generation.

However, the father/son relationship does not remain the same throughout the child's life. It changes and matures over the years. As we grow from infancy to adulthood, the relationship matures. This fact is reflected in the Scriptures. In the New Testament, there are different words translated *"son"*, each of which has its own significance. For instance, in John 1:12 we are told that *"as many as received Him, to them He gave the power to become the sons of God, even to them who believe in His name."* The word *"sons"* in that verse describes infants, or new-born children. Nobody is born as an adult. We begin small and grow toward maturity. Then, in Romans 8:14 we read: *"As many as are led by the Spirit of God, they are the sons of God."* There, *"sons"* refers to adult sons. All believers are children of God and joint heirs with Jesus Christ, but not all believers are mature sons. The process of progressing from infancy to maturity is tied up in the race that is set before us. Sometimes, the Lord has to help the process along by bringing us to the end of ourselves. In Hebrews 12:5-6, the word *"son"* means "a grown or mature son."

Back in chapter 5 the author chided his readers for their failure to grow spiritually. He said, *"By now you should have been teachers, but instead you need someone to teach you the ABCs of the faith all over again."* That can be true of us also and the Lord has to put some incentive behind us, to keep us running! It is easy to become complacent and comfortable.

"Chastening" in verse 5 means literally *"child raising."* Every day God is maturing us, helping us to grow from babyhood toward maturity in our faith. His chastening can take many forms, some of which can be very serious. David lost his first child as the result of sin and in 1 Corinthians 11, sickness, weakness and even death are mentioned as possible forms of chastening. Peter writes that a husband who fails to respect his wife is in danger of having his prayers hindered (1Peter 3:7). Failure to tithe may result in financial difficulties (Haggai 1:5-11). Businesses can fail, conflict at work or at home may erupt. Historically, national chastening has involved invasion and occupation by foreign powers. Whatever the form, chastening always seems to involve things "going wrong." It is always difficult to cope with and is always designed to bring us to the end of ourselves and cause us to turn back to the Lord. This does not indicate that every setback is chastening but on occasion God can and does use those things. If we experience trouble and are not aware that we have acted in a way that might incur God's chastening, there is no reason why we should assume that that is what it is. If we are walking with the Lord, He will make it clear if there is something that needs to be changed.

We should keep in mind that the motive for God's chastening is always His love. He is not vindictive; He does not discipline in order to punish. The punishment for our sin was borne completely by the Lord Jesus. God's chastening is entirely intended to bring us back from erroneous ways and reconcile us back to Him – for our own blessing. We do not always recognize His chastening as love. We may imagine He has forsaken us, or is angry with us, or has abandoned us to our enemies, but that is never so. We can be confident that whenever we hit trouble He is there to strengthen and encourage us. He does not always remove our problems but He will always give us the strength to bear them.

When God chastens us, He is dealing with us as adult children. Adults should be teachable. God is forming Christ in us and preparing us ultimately to reign with Him. According to these verses, we can react in three different ways – two foolish and one wise. 1. We could *despise* it (take it lightly, shrug it off and fail to recognize God's method of training us) in which case, the chastening is wasted and will achieve no worthwhile result in our lives. 2. We can *faint* under it (give up, take our marbles and go home). That is also unproductive because in that case we will have suffered the experience for nothing. 3. We can *endure* it (like Jesus endured His race). We are to consider Him, lest we become weary and faint in our minds.

Let us look at the next section as one unit. Verses 7-13:

> "*If you endure chastening, God is dealing with you as with sons; for what son is there whom a father does not chasten? 8 But if you are without chastening, of which all have become partakers, then you are illegitimate and not sons. 9 Furthermore, we have had human fathers who corrected us, and we paid them respect. Shall we not much more readily be in subjection to the Father of spirits and live? 10 For they indeed for a few days chastened us as seemed best to them, but He for our profit, that we may be partakers of His holiness. 11 Now no chastening seems to be joyful for the present, but grievous; nevertheless, afterward it yields the peaceable fruit of righteousness to those who have been trained by it.*"

Sadly, there are many parents today who do not discipline their children. The children grow up willful and rebellious because they have never been taught to respect and obey those in authority. Many of them have a rough time when they go out into the world because human employers will not accommodate their likes and dislikes in the way to which they have been accustomed at home. God acts as a loving father, who cares for and teaches his children. He acts as human fathers are expected to act, teaching and nurturing His family with His children's blessing in mind and chastening them when necessary.

It is true that we do not enjoy chastening while it lasts. I remember very vividly not enjoying discipline when it fell on me at school. However, after having paid for my misdeeds, I felt lightened and free of debt. The episode which had brought chastening upon me was now closed and I made a silent decision not to repeat the offense. The difference between this earthly discipline and God's chastening is enormous, of course. As verse 10 explains: *"They indeed for a few days chastened us as seemed best to them, but He for our profit, that we may be partakers of His holiness."* During a child's growing up years, while under his parents' discipline, the days may seem to be long. In fact they amount to "but a few days" when compared with a lifetime. God, of course, has eternal values in mind.

We should bear in mind that not all of God's chastening is grievous, just as not all the chastening by human parents involves spanking. As we noted earlier, the word translated *"chastening"* in this passage means *"child-raising."* God, as a faithful father, seeks to teach us what we should do and what we should not do.

When a Christian errs in his walk, the Holy Spirit gently convicts him of his error. Similarly, when he fails to carry out a Christian duty he is urged to take action. Since a non-believer is not indwelt by the Holy Spirit, he is unlikely to receive these corrections and the absence of such guidance would be a warning of his lost state. Certainly, some chastening is of a heavier nature but God is just and suits the discipline to the situation.

All human beings, Christians and non-Christians alike, are liable to suffer injury, sickness, grief or misfortune in this life. We should therefore not assume that every crisis we encounter is God's chastening. The Holy Spirit will communicate to us what is and what is not discipline.

Verses 12-13:

"Therefore strengthen the hands which hang down, and the feeble knees, 13 and make straight paths for your feet, so that what is lame may not be dislocated, but rather be healed."

Here are three admonitions. 1. *"Lift up your hands that hang down."* We work with our hands. There is no value in going through life with our spiritual shoulders hunched and our spiritual hands hanging at our sides. There is work to be done and God expects us all to play our part. 2. *"Strengthen the feeble knees."* We use our knees when we walk, run and jump. We cannot run the race efficiently with feeble knees. In Ephesians chapter 5 Paul tells us to "walk circumspectly" (carefully), avoiding the mud and swamps of life. 3. *"Make straight our paths."* This means that we should check our way for pits and bumps, which could cause us to stumble. These hindrances, though allegorical here, are very real in practice. Temptations, bad attitudes, resentments, feuds, dishonesty and anger all represent pitfalls along the way. We should survey our path and make sure that any hindrances have been dealt with. The word translated *"dislocated"* at the end of verse 13 is *"put out of joint"* in several modern translations and *"disabled"* in the NIV.

Pursue peace

Verse 14:

"Pursue peace with all men, and holiness, without which no one will see the Lord."

Peace with *God* is a gift possessed by every Christian. It is not something for which we have to strive; it is a gift of grace, won for us by the Lord Jesus Christ. Peace with all *men* is not the same. It is not automatically possessed by all Christians. It has to be actively pursued. Verses 1-2 of this chapter admonish us to run the race that is set before us, looking away to Jesus. Jesus is the Prince of Peace and therefore, if our focus is on Him, peace with men should be a reflection of His character. He is the great reconciler. He went to the cross specifically to make peace between man and God. A person who professes to love God but who is characterized by strife with his brother is therefore a contradiction in terms. Christians should be peacemakers, going out of their way to avoid quarrels, even if that means accepting the blame for a wrong they feel they did not commit.

Holiness means being set apart for God. Every Christian has positional holiness because Christ won it for him at the cross. In Hebrews 10:10 this is called *"sanctification"*, which is the same thing. Without it, no man will see the Lord because it is given only to those who trust Jesus Christ for salvation. It is therefore to be pursued as a precious commodity. *"Seek the Lord while He may be found. Call upon Him while He is near. Let the wicked forsake his way, and the unrighteous man his thoughts, and let him return unto the Lord. And He will have mercy; and to our God, for He will abundantly pardon."* (Isaiah 55:6-7)

Verse 15:

". . looking diligently lest anyone fall short of the grace of God; lest any root of bitterness springing up cause trouble, and by this many become defiled."

This verse follows on from the previous exhortation concerning keeping the peace, and is also frequently misunderstood. Some believe it teaches that Christians can fall away and lose their salvation, but this is certainly not its meaning. If you are a Christian, you have already been saved by God's grace. You have not fallen short of it. But there may be someone in the next pew who has never trusted Christ. He or she may have heard the way many times but has never made a commitment. They have fallen short of saving grace. This verse is an admonition to look around diligently to see if there is anyone in our circle who falls into this category.

The next question is, *"What is this root of bitterness to which the writer refers?"* The source of the expression seems to be Deuteronomy 29:18, which reads: *"Beware lest there be among you a man or woman or family or tribe, whose heart turns away this day from the Lord our God to go and serve the gods of those nations; lest there be among you a root bearing poisonous and bitter fruit."* The bitter fruit would appear to be the influence of an apostate or nonbeliever in the lives of others. As Paul wrote to the Corinthians, *"A little leaven leavens the whole lump,"* meaning that the sin of a few could contaminate many. Those who fall short of the grace of God (non believers) might possibly undermine the faith of those in their group, and should therefore be carefully nurtured.

In another sense, true believers can become bitter and disgruntled. This happens when they resent something which the Lord has allowed to come into their lives. Bitterness is a form of rebellion. Instead of keeping their eyes on the Lord, they focus on themselves, or on other people, or on their circumstances. They become angry over something they perceive to be unfair or insulting and in doing so they affect those around them. Nobody enjoys the company of bitter or resentful people. They certainly do not reflect the Lord Jesus, whom they claim to trust. Looking away to Jesus is the solution to this kind of problem. He can soften the heart and release it from the grip of anger and resentment.

Verses 16-17:

"... *lest there be any fornicator or profane person like Esau, who for one morsel of food sold his birthright. 17 For you know that afterward, when he wanted to inherit the blessing, he was rejected, for he found no place for repentance, though he sought it diligently with tears.*"

The words "*fornicator*" and "*profane*" are used here in a different sense from present normal usage. Modern translations substitute the words "*immoral*" and "*godless.*" Esau was immoral in the sense that he discounted the gift which God had given him and carelessly exchanged it for instant gratification. He was profane in the sense that he distained God's sovereign will and thought only of his own desires. Later, when his hunger had been satisfied and he realized what he had lost, he sought to reclaim his blessing, but that was not possible. (Genesis 27:30-38).

Basically, Esau's problem was self gratification. He was more interested in satisfying himself than he was in doing God's will. Many in our churches today have the same viewpoint. To them, worship is OK. They will sit through a sermon on Sunday morning and accept the routine of church life, but their real interest is in making money and achieving worldly success. True devotion to Christ is missing and God knows who they are. Jesus said that in the last day He will say to these mere professors: *"I never knew you; depart from me, you who work iniquity."* (Matthew 7:23).

Awe of God

Verses 18-21:

"For you have not come to the mountain that may be touched and that burned with fire, and to blackness and darkness and tempest, 19 and the sound of a trumpet and the voice of words, so that those who heard it begged that the word should not be spoken to them anymore. 20 (For they could not endure what was commanded: "And if so much as a beast touches the mountain, it shall be stoned or thrust through with an arrow." 21 And so terrifying was the sight that Moses said, "I am exceedingly afraid and trembling.")

The reference here, of course, is to Exodus 19, where Mount Sinai was the scene of Israel's meeting with God. The dramatic events which took place there were witnessed by the senses. The people *saw* the fire, *heard* the trumpet and *quaked* at the audible voice of God. Sinai itself was a material, touchable location, whereas the presence of the Lord today, though just as real, is entirely spiritual. Jesus told the woman at the well, *"Woman, believe me, the hour is coming when you will neither on this mountain (Mount Gerizim) nor in Jerusalem, worship the Father. . . .but the hour is coming, and now is, when the true worshippers will worship the Father in spirit and truth."* (John 4:21-23). The ancient Israelites looked back to Sinai whereas Christians look back to the cross. The point which the writer is making seems to be that the Lord is no less awesome and terrifying today than He was at Sinai. Taking Him for granted, or shrugging Him off, as is illustrated by Esau and those like him, is an extremely foolish thing to do

Verses 22-23:

"But you have come to Mount Zion and to the city of the living God, the heavenly Jerusalem, to an innumerable company of angels, 23 to the general assembly and church of the firstborn who are registered in heaven, to God the Judge of all, to the spirits of just men made perfect."

Mount Zion is one of the hills upon which Jerusalem is built, but the writer is not referring to this. He is speaking spiritually. The heavenly Jerusalem will be revealed one day, and when it is, it will be populated by the wonderful congregation of spiritual beings listed in these verses. The great body of *angels* (too many to count) will be there, shining in their veils of glory. The *Church* will be there -- the called-out ones of all ages, and of all nationalities, who have trusted Christ for salvation and have been redeemed by His blood. The babies who have died in heathen places throughout the ages will be there, together with the millions of little aborted ones from this country and around the world. The little children destroyed in the world's wars will be there, no longer as children, of course. The very word, "child" speaks of time but their souls are eternal. There will be no time and no age in the New Jerusalem. All will be transformed and shining as the sun; all of them written in the Lamb's book of life. *God, the judge of all*, will be there. Nobody will be barred from His presence. All classes of people, from princes to paupers, will enjoy an equal standing before His throne. *The spirits of just men made perfect* will be there. I believe these are the Old Testament saints, who lived in obedience to God and were faithful to as much as they knew. They looked forward to Calvary, awaiting the redemption that it would bring. Without realizing it, they anticipated the day when the risen Christ would empty sheol (hades) and lead them in triumphant procession into the presence of the Father. (Ephesians 4:8). All will join in a chorus of rapturous rejoicing.

Verse 24:

". . . to Jesus the Mediator of the new covenant, and to the blood of sprinkling that speaks better things than that of Abel."

The Savior Himself will be present among the redeemed. The *"New Covenant"* is described in Jeremiah 31:31-33 as the indwelling Christ. *"Christ in us, the hope of glory."* Such a relationship was not possible until after the atonement. Soon after the Lord's ascension into Heaven, the Holy Spirit descended and the New Covenant was ushered in. *"The blood of sprinkling"* was the price that was paid. The justice of God was satisfied and we were set forever free. In Genesis 4:10, the blood of Abel cried to God from the ground. Today, the blood of Christ cries to God on our behalf, and is a billion times more effective. According to this verse, the redeeming blood will be represented in Heaven as a token of our redemption.

Verses 25-26:

"See that you do not refuse Him who speaks. For if they did not escape who refused Him who spoke on earth, much more shall we not escape if we turn away from Him who speaks from heaven, 26 whose voice then shook the earth; but now He has promised, saying, "Yet once more I shake not only the earth, but also heaven."

If you are a Christian, you have placed your trust in the Lord Jesus Christ. You have certainly not *"refused Him."* The admonition in this verse is clearly intended as a warning to those who have not received Christ. Continuing to refuse His offer of forgiveness will have tragic results. God has always meant what He says. He meant what He said at Sinai and those who refused to obey His word died in the wilderness. All through the Old Testament, rejection of God's commands resulted in terrible judgment. Since the death and resurrection of Christ, God has spoken by different means (Hebrews 1:1-2) but He is still the same God. He has not changed in any way. *"He is the same, yesterday, today and forever."* Refusal to hear Him today will result in judgment, just as it did in the days of ancient Israel. Verses 25-26 are a stern warning against disregarding God's invitation to be saved.

Verse 27:

"Now this, "Yet once more," indicates the removal of those things that are being shaken, as of things that are made, that the things which cannot be shaken may remain."

The writer is quoting from Haggai 2:6, where God says: *"Once more (it is a little while) I will shake the heaven and earth, the sea and the dry land; and I will shake all nations, and they shall come to The Desire of All Nations, and I will fill this temple with glory."* The "Desire of All Nations" is Jesus Christ, who will one day rule in power and glory.

There is coming a day when everything we call solid (temporal) will be shaken and removed, leaving only those things which are unshakeable (eternal). Peter knew all about that future event. In his second letter he wrote: "*But the day of the Lord will come as a thief in the night, in which the heavens shall pass away with a great noise, the elements shall melt with fervent heat, the earth also. And the works that are in it shall be burned up.*" Verse 12 says, "*The heavens, being on fire, shall be dissolved, and the elements shall melt with fervent heat.*" Hebrews 1:12 speaks of the Lord Jesus folding up the created universe like a worn out garment and replacing it with a new one. That will be a shaking infinitely more cataclysmic than anything that has ever happened since the world was made. Only God could predict such an unimaginable upheaval and only God could bring it about.

What will remain when this terrible event has passed? A new world will have replaced the old. Sin and rebellion will be no more. The people of God will be free from Satan's wiles and the heavenly Jerusalem will shine in all her glory. God will make all things new. The greatest issue facing every member of the human race today is whether or not to be part of this wonderful new universe. Failure to do so will result in unending banishment from light, life and fulfillment.

Verses 28-20:

"*Therefore, since we are receiving a kingdom which cannot be shaken, let us have grace, by which we may serve God acceptably with reverence and godly fear. 29 For our God is a consuming fire.*"

The kingdom we shall one day inherit will be "for ever." The horrors of today's world, the insufferable arrogance of men and the corruption that sin has brought into God's creation will never be seen again. The earth will be filled with the glory of God as the waters cover the sea. God Himself will reign and all enemies will have been put down. Whether we are ready or not, we must all meet Him one day. There can be no avoiding that. How much better it will be to meet Him as our Father, and to live forever under His protection and love, than to meet Him as Judge. It must be one or the other. There is no third choice.

CHAPTER 13

This final chapter of Hebrews concentrates on the practical out- flowing of the Christian faith. It is not only what we believe that matters, but how we behave as well. Too many Christian testimonies are spoiled by bad or inconsiderate behavior. If we are looking to Jesus for our strength, then His characteristics should shine through. When the children were young and we attended their programs at school, we would amuse ourselves by guessing which child belonged to which parents. It was surprising how often we guessed correctly. The children did not try to look like their parents, but the parents' life was within them and the likeness was part of their being. That is how it should be with believers in Jesus Christ. His life is within us and His characteristics should show up without any effort on our part, as we stay in close fellowship with Him.

It is not surprising that the list begins with love. God *is* love and Jesus consistently stresses it. In Matthew 22, we read about a lawyer who asked Jesus which was the great commandment of the law. Jesus replied, *"You shall love the Lord your God with all your heart, with all your soul and with all your mind. This is the first and great commandment. And the second is like it: you shall love your neighbor as yourself. On these two commandments hang all the law and the prophets."* In other words, all Scripture is based upon love. John wrote in his first letter: *"He who does not love his brother, whom he has seen, how can he love God, whom he has not seen? This commandment we have from Him: that he who loves God must love his brother also."*

So – verse 1: *"**Love of the brethren**."*

"Let brotherly love continue."

The words, *"brotherly love"* are the translation of the Greek word

191

"philadelphia," which means a warm affection between brothers. "*Continue*" is "meno," which means "to abide, or to remain." This word is used well over one hundred times in the New Testament, and it always describes a settling down of something in one place. It is translated variously as "abide," "endure," "tarry," "dwell." "remain." and "continue." In other words, the writer wanted brotherly affection to be an enduring characteristic of his readers' fellowship.

Every Christian has been born spiritually into the same family – the family of God. We share the same heavenly Father, enjoy the same spiritual life and anticipate the same eternal inheritance. We are therefore truly brothers and sisters within God's spiritual household and it is His desire for us to be characterized by a sweetness and warmth which is normally experienced only within a loving family circle. I imagine we would all agree that maintaining a universal affection is easier said than done. Some people are easy to love; they seem to draw love from you. But others take a little more concentration. There are also temperaments to be considered. Some among us like to be around others and it is second nature for them to interrelate. Others are more shy and withdrawn. They find socializing more difficult.

The question therefore arises, "Does God expect us to disregard our natural makeup?" I think not. Love for our neighbor is not produced by us. It begins with God and flows to us from Him. 1 John 4:7-8 makes that very clear. It reads: "*Beloved, let us love one another: for love comes from God, and everyone who loves is born of God. He who does not love does not know God; for God is love.*" While it is true that "*love*" in that passage is not "philadelphia", but the godly "*agape*" love, I believe it takes that to produce true "*philadelphia.*" The closer we walk with the Lord, the more naturally we shall demonstrate His love to those around us. The only love worth having is His love, because it is pure, selfless and sincere. We cannot switch it on. The best we could do in our own strength is to *act* as if we loved, in which case we would merely succeed in wearing a cloak of hypocrisy, which others soon see through. People who are cold or unfriendly are sometimes selfish people, who think only of their own feelings. However, sometimes they are people who have been deeply hurt and need compassion and love to help them heal. Those who are walking with the Lord will reach out naturally, regardless of their temperament, because they will think in terms of others' needs instead of their own.

Verse 2: "***Love of strangers.***"

"Do not forget to entertain strangers, for thereby some have unwittingly entertained angels."

This refers primarily to Old Testament times, when people such as Lot and Abraham found themselves unexpectedly entertaining angels. The thrust of the sentence does not focus on the angels but on the willingness to entertain strangers. In the Old Testament accounts, the visitors were not recognized as angelic beings until after they had been received and graciously entertained. We are unlikely to repeat Abraham's experience, but one thing is certain, we shall never have the opportunity unless we are willing to take the first step.

The phrase, *"entertain strangers"* is the translation of a word which literally means *"stranger-lovers,"* and is often translated *"hospitality"* in the New Testament. Many people think that "hospitality" consists of having friends over to the house for dinner but that is not the real sense of the word. Strangers are people we do *not* know, such as visiting speakers or missionaries. In New Testament times, Christians moved from place to place to preach. Others were destitute due to persecution. There was no public assistance or welfare program to supply their needs and so they relied on fellow believers to give them food and shelter. John's third letter is built around this subject. Gaius is praised for his willingness to receive and help people in need, while Diotrephes is condemned for his selfishness. Time have changed but the principle remains the same.

In some churches, it is difficult to find lodging for visiting missionaries. People draw back and say "They are strangers; we don't know them." That is the point of this verse. It should be part of our "reasonable service" to invite visitors into our homes and to show them Christian love. They will not remain strangers for long. They will become friends, who remember with gratitude the kindness they received at our hand.

Verse 3: "***Love of the persecuted.***"

"Remember the prisoners as if chained with them, and those who are mistreated, since you yourselves are in the body also."

This is not a command to become involved in the prison ministry (though there would be nothing wrong with that). Almost certainly, this letter was written to Jewish Christians who lived in Rome. According to R. C. Lenski, the respected Lutheran scholar, the Christians who suffered so terribly during Nero's persecution were mainly members of the multi-racial Gentile body, who had been won to Christ during Paul's ministry there. Philippians 4:22 tells us that this group even included some of Nero's own household. The many Jewish Christians, on the other hand, remained separate. They continued to worship in several synagogues in and around the city. Some of these synagogues eventually became totally Christian, the non assenting members moving to other assemblies. However, because they were Jewish, and Judaism continued to be legal in Rome for the time being, these people were not molested, except when they reached out in sympathy to their mainly Gentile brothers and sisters. It was then they suffered *"reproaches and afflictions . . . . . and the spoiling of their goods."* (Hebrews 10:32-34). This letter was written primarily to these Jewish Christians, who (for the time being) were escaping the main thrust of Nero's persecution but who were tempted to re-embrace Judaism in order to escape the fate of their Gentile brothers and sisters. Here the writer says, *"Remember the prisoners, as if chained with them."* They were to remember the fact that they were one body, even though they belonged to different groups, and they were to do what they could to support and minister to those who, because of their faith, were suffering persecution.

It may be difficult for us to identify with this situation because (at present) none of our immediate number is being subjected to such affliction. Nevertheless, there are plenty of our Christian brothers and sisters, at the present time, who are being persecuted in other parts of the world. We should remember them in prayer, and minister to them in whatever way we can, bearing in mind that they are guilty of nothing more than we are guilty of ourselves, namely, of trusting Jesus Christ as our Lord and Savior.

Verse 4: "*Love of marriage partners*."

"Marriage is honorable among all, and the bed undefiled; but fornicators and adulterers God will judge."

This is a command, not a statement. It should read, *"Let marriage be honored by all, and let the bed be undefiled, for fornicators and adulterers God will judge."* God designed marriage in the first place and there is nothing unclean or ungodly in any part of the marriage relationship. Man did not invent the desires that consummate the marriage union; God did. Without them the human race would cease to exist. But like anything else, when man takes a godly thing out of context and uses it illicitly G228 to gratify his own lusts, it becomes bad. Sex is the number one area of such abuse.

I find it difficult to understand how so many professing Christians can stand at the altar on their wedding day and solemnly swear to be faithful and true to one another for the remainder of their lives, calling upon God to be a witness to their vows, and then go out and have an affair with somebody else. I hear the same excuses that you do: that they were swept off their feet, that they fell in love, that their partner was not meeting their needs, and so on. These may be excuses but they are not reasons. The reason for their adultery is lack of integrity – a selfish desire to gratify the lusts of their flesh and a flagrant disregard for the promises they made to their spouse and to God on their wedding day. Modern society accepts this behavior but here we see that God does not. He will judge it.

Jesus deepened the subject considerably when He said, *"You have heard that it was said by them of old time, "You shall not commit adultery." But I say to you that whosoever looks on a woman to lust after her has committed adultery with her already in his heart."* His statement takes adultery out of the purely physical category and makes it mental. In doing this, many more people become guilty because now the sin can be committed in secret and only God is privy to it.

Obviously, adultery is not an unpardonable sin. 1 John 1:9 still applies. Forgiveness and cleansing can still be found through true repentance, but the scars remain and will probably damage the relationship permanently. God takes marriage very seriously and He expects us to take it seriously as well. Marriage is a picture of Christ and the church. Unfaithfulness within the marriage affronts Him.

Verses 5-6: "***Love of money.***"

"*Let your conduct be without covetousness, and be content with such things as you have. For He Himself has said, "I will never leave you nor forsake you. 6 So we may boldly say: "The Lord is my helper; I will not fear. What can man do to me?"*

"*Covetousness*" is another compound. In verse 1 we had "*love of brother,*" in verse 2 we had "*love of stranger,*" and here in verse 5 we have "*love of money.*" The only difference is that this one has an alpha attached to it, which turns it into a negative –"*Without* love of money." Greed is offensive to God. It says, in effect, that God is not sufficient to supply our needs. Paul told Timothy:

"*Godliness with contentment is great gain (for we brought nothing into this world, and it is certain we shall carry nothing out). So, having food and clothing, let us therewith be content.*" (1 Timothy 6:8).

However, food and clothing alone do not bring us contentment. True contentment is spiritual in nature. It springs from the sure knowledge that Christ is forever and irrevocably committed to His people. In the original, there are two negatives before "*leave*" (verse 6) and three negatives before "*forsake.*" ("*I will never, never leave you; I will not, will not, will not forsake you.*") That is about as absolute a guarantee of His unfailing faithfulness as it is possible to have. It is that awareness which produces true contentment. Every Christian possesses that guarantee but not every Christian reckons on it. Consequently, not all Christians are content. It we look for "things" to bring us satisfaction, we shall remain discontented. Some of the richest people in the world have been the most discontented and some of the most contented have been among the poorest. Contentment comes with commitment – with the recognition that our lives are in the Lord's hands and that He will never let us down.

These Hebrew Christians were living in the shadow of terrible atrocities.

They knew that at any moment Nero's mob might come after them. Those who were dying were condemned for having the same faith as they had. The pressure must have been intense. But here, the writer tells them, *"He will never, never leave you; He will never, never, never forsake you. Therefore you can boldly say, 'The Lord is my helper, and I will not fear what man can do to me.'"* What could man do to them? He could throw them to the lions or the wild dogs in the arena; he could cover them with pitch and use them as torches to illuminate the games; he could crucify them like Peter, or behead them like Paul. What kind of faith did they need to be unafraid of that kind of cruelty? We shall never know how faith comes unless we are called upon to face the same kind of thing. God gives strength when it is needed, not before.

Respect for authority

Verse 7:

"Remember those who rule over you, who have spoken the word of God to you, whose faith follow, considering the outcome of their conduct."

In this section, the writer stresses the need for stability in our faith and approaches it from two or three different angles. This first angle has to do with the past. At first glance, we might assume that verse 7 refers to the Hebrews' present leaders, but the grammar of the text makes it clear that the writer was referring to past teachers, who had originally taught them the word of God and had provided them with the foundation upon which their faith had been built. Most of us can look back to people who did the same for us. If we are strong in our faith today, it is more than likely that someone in the past grounded us faithfully in the word of God. For me it was Alan Redpath and John Hunter and I look back on them both with great respect and gratitude. God used them to open my eyes to truths I may otherwise never have seen – precious truths that provided a foundation upon which everything else was built. If I was ever tempted to waver it would be to them that my mind would turn. What did they teach me? How did they live? What did they base their lives upon?

Different translations render the words *"considering the end of their conversation*" (KJV) (at the end of verse 7) in more or less the same way. The NKJV says, "*considering the outcome of their conduct.*" The NASB says, "*considering the result of their conduct.*" The NIV says, "*considering the outcome of their way of life.*" These are all correct but what did the writer mean by his statement? What *was* the outcome of their way of life? As I look back on the men who had the greatest influence in my developing faith, the thrust of their teaching and the focus of their lives is perfectly summed up in the next verse.

Verse 8:

"*Jesus Christ is the same yesterday, today, and forever.*"

That is the truth which their lives and teaching impressed upon me. I believe it was this that the writer to the Hebrews intended to convey to his readers – that we should remember the truth that our mentors gave us; that Jesus Christ alone must be the foundation, focus and fulfillment of our faith. Jesus does not change. Circumstances change, fashions change, fads come and go but Jesus Christ remains the same. There is no shadow of turning in Him. Not only is He personally changeless, but His victory is changeless also. No matter what happens in this world, no matter what course history may take, the fact of Christ's atonement remains inviolate. This truth must be the unshakeable foundation of our faith. As Paul told the Corinthians: "*No other foundation can anyone lay but that which is laid, which is Jesus Christ.*" (1 Corinthians 3:11).

Remain true to the Word

Verse 9:

"*Be not carried about with various and strange doctrines. For it is good that the heart be established by grace, not with foods which have not profited those who have been occupied with them.*"

"Doctrines," of course, are teachings. "Strange" teachings are those which do not conform to the clear teaching of Scripture. In the days when this letter was written, the principal danger was that of reverting to the legalistic system associated with Old Testament worship, involving food laws and strict observances. That is no longer a danger for most people but today the air continues to be full of teaching that is "strange" as far as the Scriptures are concerned. This teaching may sound reasonable enough to human logic, but if it contradicts or adds to the clear truth of Scripture it is "strange" and should be avoided. The Bible is a unit. It does not contradict itself. There is one clear flow of doctrine throughout the Scriptures. 1 Timothy 3 summarizes it:

"All Scripture is given by inspiration of God (God breathed), and is profitable for doctrine. for reproof, for correction, for instruction in righteousness: that the man of God may be perfect (complete), thoroughly equipped for every good work."

In other words, since God Himself inspired what the original writers wrote, then the teaching, reproof, correction and instruction found within their work originated with God. Any teaching that contradicts what the Bible says disregards the inspiration and wisdom of God Himself. Any teaching, no matter how convincing it seems to be, that claims:

A. that the Bible is not the Word of God;

B. that the Lord Jesus is not God;

C. that Christ is not the only way to salvation,

-- is "strange" and should be disregarded. In Galatians 1, Paul writes:

"Even if we, or an angel from Heaven, preach any other Gospel to you than what we have preached, let him be accursed. As we have said before, so now I say again, if anyone preaches any other Gospel to you than what you have received, let him be accursed."

The true sacrifice

Verse 10:

"We have an altar from which those who serve the tabernacle have no right to eat."

The people who served the tabernacle were the priests. They had the God-given right to eat some of the meat that was offered on the altar of sacrifice. That was their privilege. It was given to them by reason of their office, or calling. As Christians, we do not need priests anymore.

They were made redundant by the sacrifice of Jesus. We may now come directly to God through Jesus Christ and the "altar" to which we look for our right of access is not made of bronze, upon which animals are slain; it is a cross of wood, where the Lamb of God died as our substitute. The priests, who served the tabernacle and temple, did not inherit the right, by reason of their office, to approach the cross. They could approach it like everybody else, but only as guilty sinners in need of cleansing. All men were now brought to the same level and given the same opportunity. The cross was an altar of rejection and cursing. To the Jews it was a stumbling block, to the Greeks, it was foolishness, but to those are called, both Jews and Greeks, it is the emblem of atonement.

Verses 11-14:

"For the bodies of those beasts, whose blood is brought into the sanctuary by the high priest for sin, are burned outside the camp. 12 Therefore Jesus also, that He might sanctify the people with His own blood, suffered outside the gate. 13 Therefore let us go forth to Him, outside the camp, bearing His reproach. 14 For here we have no continuing city, but we seek the one to come."

The Christian's altar (the cross) is a picture of the sacrifice on the great Day of Atonement. On that day, the priests were not allowed to eat any of it. The sacrifice was made at the altar, the blood was sprinkled on the Mercy Seat, within the veil, to atone for the sins of the people, and then the bodies of the animals slain were taken outside the camp and burned there. In the wilderness days, "the camp" meant Israel. The sacrifice was rejected and thrust away. In the days of Jesus there was no longer a camp but there was a city. Jesus, the Savior, was thrust out of the city and crucified on a plot of land outside the wall. This is being used as an analogy. The Hebrew readers are being encouraged to leave behind the bondage of the law (to leave the camp, so to speak) and to follow Jesus outside, bearing His reproach. We are all asked to do that.

In the present day, "Religion" is still quite popular, but Jesus is not. You may talk about "church", or "religion", even "God," without engendering much opposition, but speak about Jesus and the people around you will become uncomfortable, embarrassed or hostile. However, the Bible demands that we identify with Jesus, even in His rejection. This may result in our being rejected also but that is the price we have to pay. Any teaching that changes or ignores the centrality of Christ is "strange" and must be rejected as false.

We should not be confused by the word "*city*" in verse 14. The writer is continuing his picture of Christ being thrust outside the Jerusalem city gate to die, and of our willingness to be rejected along with Him. No particular city is in view, but rather a settled dwelling place. This world is not our home; we are citizens of Heaven. Therefore we should not be surprised if we do not fit into the world's philosophy. We are foreigners and strangers and do not belong here. Paul spoke of having a desire to leave this world and be present with Chris, but he wanted to remain as long as God deemed fit because he knew he still had work to do.

Verse 15:

"Therefore by Him let us continually offer the sacrifice of praise to God, that is, the fruit of our lips, giving thanks to His name."

"Sacrifice" carries the sense of deliberately forfeiting one thing for the sake of something else. When a soldier sacrifices his life for his country, he willingly relinquishes it in order that his country might benefit. It can also be the price paid for a greater benefit. Always it stands for the forfeiture of something valuable for the sake of something else. That being the case, praise might seem to be a strange sacrifice. Surely we give up very little in order to offer God our praise. However, in order to genuinely praise Him, we must place Him first on our list of priorities. This, in turn, means denying self. The sacrifice then becomes self-will and self-interest, which are far more precious to us than we may imagine. It is easy to sing songs of praise, or to speak words of adoration. They cost us nothing. Unless our hearts and lives back up what we sing or say, our "praise" is empty. Jesus said, *"You hypocrites, well did Isaiah prophesy to you, saying, This people draws near to me with their lips; but their heart is far from me. In vain do they worship me, teaching for doctrines the commandments of men."* (Matthew 15:7-9). We are therefore admonished to offer true worship.

"Giving thanks" falls into the same category. It is more or less natural to give thanks for large or miraculous blessings. When something special happens we feel grateful and find it easy to give thanks. However, we tend to take many everyday blessings for granted. The blessings of health, family, home, food, water, clothing and transportation all come from the Lord. James, the Lord's brother, wrote: *"Every good gift and every perfect gift is from above, and comes down from the Father of light, with whom is no variableness, neither shadow of turning."* (James 1:17). True thanksgiving recognizes our total dependence upon Him and recognizes that He is the source of every blessing, great and small.

Verse 16:

"But do not forget to do good and to share, for with such sacrifices God is well pleased."

A willingness to share what we have with others is well-pleasing to God. Selfishness never is. Selfishness places self before God and tends to overlook the fact that all we have belongs to Him anyway. When I was a child, I remember our pastor asking the blessing on the church offering and using a verse from a hymn by C.W. Poole:

"We give Thee but Thine own,
Whate'er the gift may be;
All that we have is Thine alone,
A trust, O Lord, from Thee."

If our hearts are right and we give out of love for the Lord, He will ensure that our own needs are always met. 2 Corinthians 9:6-8 says: *"And God is able to make all grace abound toward you; that you, always having all sufficiency in all things, may abound to every good work."*

Obedience to those in authority

Verse 17:

"Obey those who rule over you, and be submissive, for they watch out for your souls, as those who must give account. Let them do so with joy and not with grief, for that would be unprofitable for you."

The writer was referring to those who had the oversight of the church.

These would have been the pastor and elders. They were responsible for the spiritual welfare of the believers in their care. Church oversight was not always an easy task because, in any body, even today, there are those who are not easily led. The writer to the Hebrews knew this and exhorted his readers to submit to their elders' rule. They were living in difficult times and their welfare rested largely on the maintenance of unity within the body. The elders needed wisdom in carrying out their responsibilities and therefore they relied on the support and prayers of the congregation.

Nothing much has changed through the centuries. We live today in a rebellious age, in which respect for authority is very low. Nobody wants to be told what to do. Society is pervaded by a spirit of rebellion, which, though fashionable, is certainly not from God. God places it on the same level as witchcraft! Cheerful submission to the elders' authority is as important in the present age as it was in the early church. Views, tastes and opinions abound. We all have them. However, we should remember that God holds the elders responsible for the spiritual welfare of the church, not individual members of the congregation. If there is a question, it should be taken to the elders and left there. Talking about it with other members only causes unrest and the whole church suffers. Such behavior is carnal. There is no place for politics within the local church.

Prayer requested

Verses 18-19:

"Pray for us; for we are confident that we have a good conscience, in all things desiring to live honorably. 19 But I especially urge you to do this, that I may be restored to you the sooner."

This is one of the verses in Hebrews that make people believe the writer was Paul, though there is no real evidence that it was. The words "us" and "we" in verse 18 make it clear that the writer was not alone, but the singular "I" suggests that he was planning to leave his companions when he returned to his readers. Whether he was in prison or away on some assignment will never be known. One thing is certain; had the Holy Spirit intended us to know these things He would have made them clear to us. As it is, He chose to keep the facts obscured. Psalm 84:11 says, *"No good thing will he withhold."* Therefore we must assume that knowledge of all the details would have done us no good anyway.

Benediction

Verses 20-21:

"Now may the God of peace who brought up our Lord Jesus from the dead, that great Shepherd of the sheep, through the blood of the everlasting covenant, 21 make you complete in every good work to do His will, working in you what is well pleasing in His sight, through Jesus Christ, to whom be glory forever and ever. Amen."

Here is one of the most beautiful benedictions to be found in the Scriptures. Taken as a whole, it is lengthy and rather involved but when broken down into its parts, it becomes clear. Once the central statement is isolated, the remainder of the paragraph consists of descriptive clauses, which tell us how and through whom God may achieve the central goal.

The central statement is simply *"God"* (at the beginning of verse 20) . . . *."make you complete"* (the beginning of verse 21). The KJV has *"perfect"* in place of *"complete"*; the NASB and the NIV both have *"equip you in every good thing,"* but the sense in each case is the same. The writer was praying that his readers would become mature in their faith and be able to withstand the pressures of a godless society. Spiritual maturity is only experienced through the agency of the Holy Spirit. These Hebrews already had the Spirit dwelling within them. Thus, they already had all the equipment they needed – just as you and I do. Where spiritual immaturity exists, the cause is never with the Lord. It is always with the Christian, who has failed to allow God to have His way.

A common problem with Christians is that many do not understand what spiritual maturity is. Some imagine that it is knowing the Bible from front to back, or committing large portions of it to memory, or visiting the sick. Others believe it involves attending every meeting at church, praying or giving to missions. All these things are good but none of them amounts to spiritual maturity. Spiritual maturity is reached when we come to a place in our lives when we truly believe that we possess neither the wisdom nor the ability to run things on our own; when we finally give in and allow God to control every aspect of our lives; when we are willing to relinquish control of our private affairs and our church affairs into His hands. The more assertive we become, the weaker we grow; the more we rely upon the Lord, the stronger we become spiritually. The principal thrust of this benediction is therefore that its readers would become more and more dependent upon the Lord and less dependent upon themselves.

The remainder of the paragraph is comprised of clauses which answer the question, "*What God*?" The first answer is "**The God of Peace**." He is the God who *made* peace. He brought it about. In His love, He reached down to a lost and fallen race and brought about reconciliation through the cross. He is also the God who *gives* peace. As we surrender to Him, He replaces the old fears and anxieties with assurance.

> *"Be anxious for nothing; but in everything by prayer and supplication with thanksgiving let your requests be made known unto God, and the peace of God which passes all understanding, shall keep your hearts and minds through Christ Jesus."* (Philippians 4:6-7).

The second answer is "**The God of Power**." (He "*brought again our Lord Jesus from the dead*.") The power of the resurrection was greater than that extended to create the universe. It was the ultimate demonstration of God's sovereignty over Satan, sin and death. Prior to the resurrection, death was the final victor but now life, personified in the person of the Lord Jesus, was forever dominant. Paul prayed for the Ephesians, that they might know "*what is the exceeding greatness of His power to us-ward who believe, according to the working of His mighty power, which He wrought in Christ when He raised Him from the dead, and set Him at His own right hand in the heavenly places.*"

The third answer is "**The God of Provision**." (He is "*That great shepherd of the sheep*.") The whole idea of a shepherd is of one who provides and protects. The shepherd lives with his sheep, leads them to pasture and water, binds up their wounds and protects them from robbers and wolves. Jesus is called "the shepherd of the sheep" in the Scriptures. In Psalm 23, He is called simply, "shepherd." In John 10 He calls Himself "the *good* shepherd." Here, in Hebrews 13:20 He is called "The *great* shepherd" and in 1 Peter 5 He is called "The *chief* shepherd." He leads, guides and provides for His sheep and spiritual maturity amounts to a willingness to trust Him to do His work

The fourth answer is "**The God of Promise**." ("*Through the blood of the everlasting covenant.*") A covenant is an agreement or a promise. God's covenants fall into two categories. Some are conditional, meaning that their fulfillment depends on man's participation. Others are unconditional, wherein man plays no part in their performance. The covenant God made with Noah, for instance, was unconditional. God said, "*While the earth remains, seed-time and harvest, and cold and heat, and summer and winter, and day and night, shall not cease.*" Despite man's continued sin, we still see the rainbow today as evidence of God's promise. On the other hand, God's covenant with Solomon required the cooperation of man. God said, "*If my people, who are called by my name, will humble themselves and pray, and seek my face, and turn from their wicked ways, then I will hear from heaven, and will forgive their sin, and will heal their land.*" Clearly, the blessing would come in response to man's repentance.

However, that which is called here "*The everlasting covenant*" was not made between God and man at all. It was made between the Persons of the Godhead. The plan of salvation was settled before the earth was formed, before man sinned. It was everlasting. Christ was the "*Lamb slain from the foundation of the world.*" When Adam sinned in the Garden of Eden, the way of salvation had already been planned, the cross settled, the Christmas and Easter stories already written. It was simply a matter of time before the conditions of the Everlasting Covenant were set in motion.

The peace, the power and the provision of God, which we found in the first three clauses all depend upon the fourth: "*The blood of the everlasting covenant.*" This is the key and foundation of every Biblical doctrine, and all the clauses are brought to bear on that one goal – that you and I should be equipped for every good work, that we should fulfill the purpose for which we were saved.

The remainder of this benediction (in verse 21) answers a second question: "*How will this spiritual maturity manifest itself?*" If I have it, how will it be evidenced? The answer falls into two main sections. The first tells us "*what*" and the second tells us "*how*." The "what" of spiritual maturity is simply obedience to God's will ("*make you perfect in every good work to do His will.*") Spiritual maturity will result in obedience. Jesus was the ultimate example of this. In John 4:34 He said: "*My meat is to do the will of Him who sent me.*" In John 5:30 He said: "*I seek not my own will, but the will of the Father who sent me.*" Again, in John 6:30 He said: "*I came down from heaven, not to do my own will, but the will of Him who sent me.*" Finally, in the Garden of Gethsemane, just before His arrest, Jesus prayed: "*If you are willing, remove this cup from me. Nevertheless, not my will but thine be done.*" In other words, Jesus (who was the ultimate in spiritual maturity) demonstrated it by His willingness to do the Father's will without complaint or question. The same would be true of the spiritually mature Christian.

In order to do the will of another there has to be submission, and submission presupposes meekness. It also presupposes trust in the one to whom submission is made. If you don't trust someone, you are unlikely to submit to him willingly. God does not force anyone to submit to His will. He desires a willing and voluntary submission.

The next clause in verse 21 takes us a step deeper: ("*. . .working in you that which is well-pleasing in His sight.*") Doing God's will is not the result of hard work on our part but the demonstration of His power working within us. Provided we are trusting and submissive to God's will, the Holy Spirit brings forth the right attitudes and actions from inside. The believer is not left to search for God's will, using some secret and mysterious process. Neither is he left to carry it out in the energy of the flesh, to "do it for God." When we submit to Him *He* will do it for *us*. It is the God of peace, power, provision and promise who works in you that which is pleasing in His sight. How? Verse 21 again: "*through Jesus Christ.*" It always comes back to Him because He is the only mediator between God and man. Without Him, nothing worthwhile is ever achieved.

And so the benediction closes with a logical burst of praise to this One who is all in all: ("*To Him be glory forever and ever, Amen.*")

Accept instruction

Verse22:

"And I appeal to you, brethren, bear with the word of exhortation, for I have written to you in few words."

"Bear" means *"endure patiently."* Sometimes the Word of God cuts. It is not always comfortable to read; it does not say what we would like it to say. I have known people leave our church because they objected to what the Bible says. However, we reject it at our peril. I imagine some of the original readers of this letter were not pleased with what they read, but it was written for their eternal benefit. Consequently, the writer exhorts them to *"endure it patiently."* We need to do the same. It is the Word of God; it is the word of life. It may call upon us to change our ways and alter our attitudes. It may put a finger on areas which are sensitive, but we can be sure that if there is a discrepancy between what it says and how we live, the fault is ours. Solomon said, *"There is a way that seems right to man, but the end thereof are the ways of death."* (Proverbs 14:12). Human logic is a God-given gift for which we should be grateful. But it is faulty, and if we base our lives upon it we could find ourselves in serious trouble.

Verse 23:

"Know that our brother Timothy has been set free, with whom I shall see you if he comes shortly."

This verse helps to convince some commentators that the writer of this epistle was Paul. Certainly the way the writer refers to Timothy suggests a Pauline authorship but there is no evidence in the statement that would confirm that belief. We are not told anywhere else about Timothy's imprisonment, which leads some to assume that he was confined in Rome with Paul. Others claim that Paul was dead when this letter was written. The best explanation amounts only to theory. Whoever the writer was, he appears to be out of prison himself, expecting Timothy to accompany him to the recipients of this letter. That is all we can claim with certainty.

Greetings

Verses 24-25

"Greet all those who rule over you, and all the saints. Those from Italy greet you. 25 Grace be with you all. Amen."

Special greetings were sent to the leaders of the church and to the congregation in general. *"Those from Italy"* were not necessarily residing *in* Italy. Those who subscribe to the Pauline authorship of Hebrews assume that the author was referring to Christians in Rome, but once again, there is nothing to support this view. The writer could quite easily have been living outside Italy, with Italian friends, awaiting Timothy to join him before embarking on his journey. *"Grace"* is the grace of God, of course; the undeserved favor and support of the Almighty toward guilty sinners. *"Amen"* (so be it) seals the epistle as a finished work.

———————

The epistle to the Hebrews is rather heavy in some places, but it also contains some of the most constructive and beneficial passages to be found in the Scriptures. As is true of all Scripture, it will benefit us greatly provided we take it seriously and hide its instruction in our hearts. If we nod approvingly and set it aside, we shall benefit from it not at all. The wise man will therefore turn it over to the Holy Spirit (the greatest teacher of all) and ask Him to make the truth of His Word come alive.

Other Books by Ashley Day

Exploring the Lives of the Patriarchs

Exploring Daniel

Exploring Isaiah

Exploring John's Gospel

Exploring Romans

Exploring 1 Corinthians

Exploring Galatians

Exploring Ephesians

Exploring Colossians

Exploring Revelation

What We Believe and Why

Saved to Serve

Copies of these books may be purchased through the publisher (Authorhouse, Tel: 800-839-8640), from Seed-Time Ministries, 5350 N, 4th Street, Coeur d'Alene, ID 83815, Tel: 208-765-3714, or from the website at http://www.seedtime.net